WOMEN'S TALES: Four Leading Israeli Jewelers

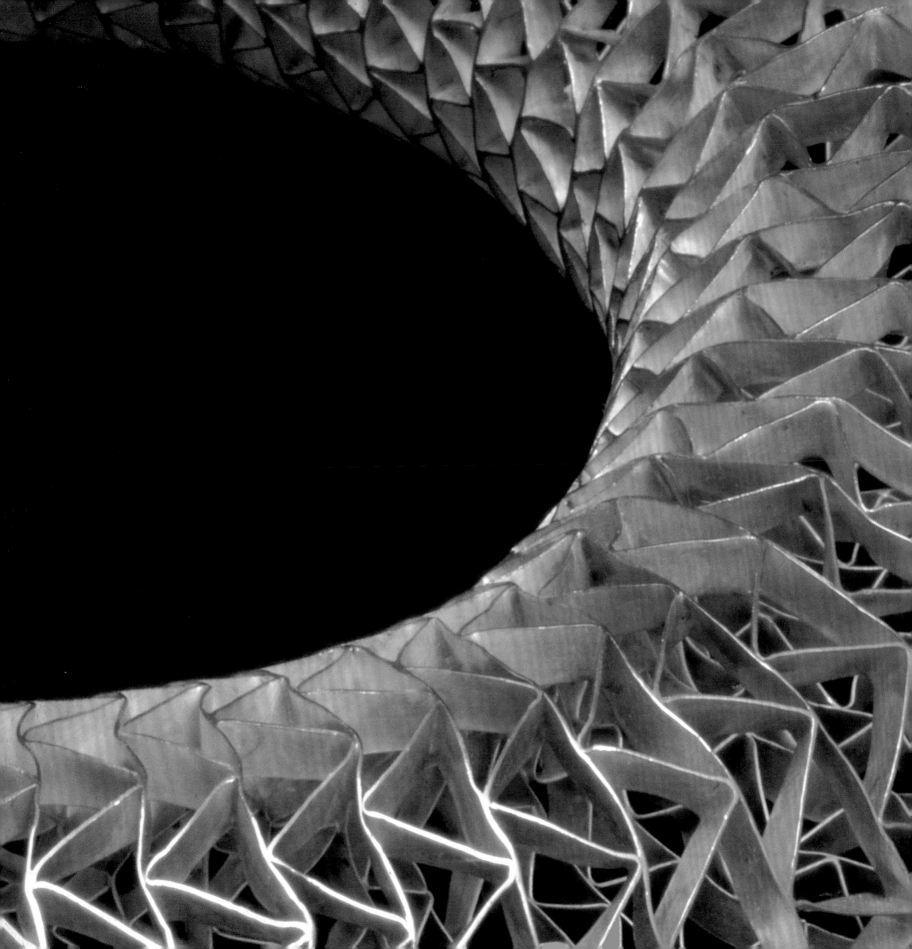

WOMEN'S TALES: Four Leading Israeli Jewelers

Davira S. Taragin and Alex Ward
with Helen W. Drutt English

The Israel Museum, Jerusalem, and
the Racine Art Museum

in association with Hudson Hills Press,
New York and Manchester

First Edition
Copyright ©2006 Racine Art Museum

Published in the United States by Hudson Hills Press LLC, 74–2 Union Street, Manchester, Vermont 05254. Distributed in the United States, its territories and posses-sions, and Canada by National Book Network, Inc. Distributed in the United Kingdom, Eire, and Europe by Windsor Books International.

Co-Directors: Leslie van Breen and Randall Perkins
Founding Publisher: Paul Anbinder

Coordinator and Editor: Terry Ann R. Neff, t.a. neff associates, inc., Tucson, Arizona
Designer: Susan Evans, Design per se, New York
Proofreader: Margot Page
Production Manager: David Skolkin/Skolkin + Chickey, Santa Fe, New Mexico

Photography by Michael Tropea, Chicago, except for EK cat. nos. 8 and 9, by Design Partners Inc., Racine, WI
Color separations by Pre Tech Color, Wilder, Vermont
Printed and bound by Oceanic Graphic Printing, China

Library of Congress Cataloging-in-Publication Data

Taragin, Davira Spiro.
  Women's tales : four leading Israeli jewelers / Davira S. Taragin and Alex Ward, with Helen W. Drutt English. — 1st ed.
    p. cm.
  Published to accompany an exhibition held at the Racine Art Museum between Sept. 17, 2006 and January 21, 2007. The exhibition will tour in Europe during 2008–2009 and be on view at The Israel Museum, Jerusalem, during 2009–2010.
  ISBN-13: 978-1-55595-270-9 (alk. paper)
  ISBN-10: 1-55595-270-4 (alk. paper)
  1. Jewelry—Israel—Exhibitions. 2. Art metal-work—Israel—Exhibitions. 3. Women jewelers—Israel—Exhibitions. I. Ward, Alex. II. Drutt English, Helen Williams. III. Racine Art Museum. IV. Muze'on Yisra'el (Jerusalem). V. Title.
  NK7373.7.A1T37 2006
  739.27095694'074—dc22
                    2006016695

This publication celebrates the exhibition *Women's Tales: Four Leading Israeli Jewelers*, organized by The Israel Museum, Jerusalem, and the Racine Art Museum, Wisconsin, on view from September 17, 2006 through January 21, 2007 in Racine, and traveling to the Bellevue Arts Museum, Washington, from March 8 through June 17, 2007; the Houston Center for Contemporary Craft from October 5, 2007 through January 6, 2008; and The Newark Museum, New Jersey, from March 19, 2008 through June 25, 2008. The exhibition will tour in Europe during 2008–2009 and be on view at The Israel Museum, Jerusalem, during 2009–2010.

The Israel Museum, Jerusalem, and the Racine Art Museum are grateful to the following sponsors:

Association of Israel's Decorative Arts (AIDA). AIDA was founded by Dale and Doug Anderson and Andrea and Charles Bronfman to foster the development of contemporary deco-rative artists from Israel by connecting them to an interna-tional audience of galleries, institutions, and collectors.

International Partnerships Among Museums (IPAM). The IPAM program is administered by the American Association of Museums (AAM) and funded by the Department of State's Bureau of Educational and Cultural Affairs (ECA).

The Racine Community Foundation

Karen and William Boyd

Elwood Corporation

Doron and Marianne Livnat, Holland

Jewish United Fund/Jewish Federation of Metropolitan Chicago

SC Johnson

Wisconsin Arts Board with funds from the State of Wisconsin

Racine United Arts Fund

Members of the RAM Society and other donors to the Racine Art Museum

Cover: Esther Knobel, *Daisy Wire*, 1993 (EK cat. no. 22)

Photograph pp. 2–3: Vered Kaminski, *Bracelet*, 1987 (VK cat. no. 3)

Photograph pp. 12–13: Bianca Eshel-Gershuni, *Necklace*, 1971 (BE-G cat. no. 5)

Photograph pp. 32–33: Deganit Stern Schocken, *City*, 2003 from *How Many Is One*, 2003–2004 (DSS cat. no. 29)

WOMEN'S TALES: Four Leading Israeli Jewelers

This exhibition and publication are dedicated to the memory of Andrea Bronfman,
whose devotion to Israel and to the advancement of the fields of contemporary art and craft
in Israel lies at the heart of this collaboration.

Foreword

Jewelry is one of the most ancient forms of decorative art. Although it is not clear precisely how this craft emerged, we know that prehistoric men and women made and wore jewelry, whether to enhance their beauty or to protect themselves, by means of amulets, from frightening ills and evils. Over the centuries, jewelry crafted from gold and precious stones came to be highly valued as a status symbol and as an indication of wealth. But in the second half of the last century, jewelry makers began to rethink their tradition and to produce radically different work, in which the expression of ideas frequently superseded purely aesthetic concerns, and new and often surprising materials replaced expensive metals and gems. And personal and cultural narratives have now found their place in the practice of jewelry making. At the same time, in this field—as in so many other spheres—geographical and geopolitical boundaries are disappearing.

It is a great pleasure for the Israel Museum to join forces with the Racine Art Museum on a project that also crosses boundaries, offering a first opportunity for the American public to see the work of four important Israeli jewelry makers. Each of the artists represented in this exhibition and publication *Women's Tales* is a leader in the field in Israel and has also been influenced by and participatory in the evolution of the craft in Europe in recent decades. All have served as curators of the biennial for Israeli jewelry at the Eretz Israel Museum, Tel Aviv, and over the years the Israel Museum has highlighted the work of three in solo exhibitions: "Bianca Eshel-Gershuni, Jewelry" (1977); "Vered Kaminski: New Objects and Jewelry" (1991); and "Refined Imagination: Esther Knobel, Jewelry" (1995). Thanks to this collaborative venture with RAM, the work of these four women, already well recognized in Israel and in Europe, will also receive the exposure it merits in North America. And for us in the Israel

Museum—whose encyclopedic collections range from the earliest objects unearthed by historical archaeologists to contemporary art and design, and represent the broad diversity of world cultures, including examples of jewelry over the millennia and from cultures around the world—there could not be a more appropriate project.

The support and promotion of the crafts in Israel is a subject very dear to the generous friends who have encouraged this collaboration—Dale and Doug Anderson and Andrea and Charles Bronfman—and to them we offer our warmest thanks and the shared hope that this enterprise will make a significant contribution to advancing international recognition of Israeli craft. We are grateful to our colleagues at the exhibition's tour venues, who are making it possible to present the exhibition across America, and our special thanks go to the Racine Art Museum and to Bruce W. Pepich, Executive Director and Curator of Collections, and to Davira S. Taragin, Director of Exhibitions and Programs, the exhibition's co-curator. Finally, we acknowledge the professional efforts of those at the Israel Museum who were involved in this project, and especially the dedicated work of Alex Ward, Curator of Design and Architecture, without whom this enterprise could not have been realized.

James S. Snyder, *Anne and Jerome Fisher Director*
The Israel Museum, Jerusalem

7

Foreword

Organized in a changing world, the exhibition "Women's Tales: Four Leading Israeli Jewelers" brings both a sense of the new and a feeling of continuum to the Racine Art Museum and its exhibition program. As a fine arts museum with a strong focus on contemporary crafts, RAM's presentation of this project falls within its ongoing efforts to augment, interpret, and contextualize its collections. Since the early 1990s, RAM has been building its contemporary metalwork collection. Like most American museums, until recently it has concentrated primarily on American jewelry rather than European developments or hollowware and architectural metalwork. The jewelry that it has chosen to acquire is primarily American work after the 1970s, which emphasizes strong sculptural statements that are figurative and narrative, and employ natural and industrial materials rather than precious stones. Within the past year, through the support of the Association of Israel's Decorative Arts (AIDA) and long-time friends of the museum, RAM has begun to expand its jewelry collection to include emerging Israeli talent.

As the first international exhibition initiated by RAM, "Women's Tales: Four Leading Israeli Jewelers" marks the beginning of a program that will attempt to place RAM's collection of primarily American crafts within an international context. This series of exhibitions will provide in-depth documentation of developments abroad that have never received critical attention but that in some way augment or amplify America's contemporary crafts aesthetic and, thus, provide an environment in which to examine global issues being addressed by artists working in craft media today. In fact, the idea for this exhibition and direction emerged during the organization of RAM's inaugural exhibition in May 2003: as Director of Exhibitions and Programs Davira S. Taragin researched a cohesive theme to unveil RAM's jewelry collection, she became aware of the void in contemporary scholarship on Israeli jewelry.

This exhibition is particularly fortuitous because it coincides with a period when Israel is considering not only its present and future but recognizing the importance of its recent past. Israeli contemporary decorative arts and crafts are also being introduced for the first time to American audiences through the efforts of the Association of Israel's Decorative Arts (AIDA). I want to thank Dale and Doug Anderson and Andrea and Charles Bronfman for all their wonderful work through numerous venues to expand our nation's awareness of this innovative work. On a personal level, I want to express our warmest appreciation to them for working with RAM on an ongoing basis to make this exhibition and the American tour possible. Their vehicle, AIDA, has most generously provided a challenge grant for this project. I would like to acknowledge the generosity of the individuals, businesses, foundations, and organizations in Racine, in the region, and beyond that have supported this exhibition. I thank all our donors, especially the major contributors listed in the front of this publication, for enabling us to meet this challenge.

I want to salute the curators for the exhibition, Davira S. Taragin and Alex Ward, Curator of Design and Architecture, The Israel Museum, Jerusalem, for the dedication and spirit with which they have addressed this subject. I thank Davira for her expertise and enthusiasm for the work of these artists; her commitment has served as an inspiration to me. Davira and I would like to extend special thanks to Terry Ann R. Neff, who provided much appreciated direction and counsel on issues well beyond catalogue conceptualization, content, and production. Similarly, we want to warmly thank Helen W. Drutt English, who has been an inspiration and a friend during critical moments in this endeavor. We also would like to extend deep appreciation to James S. Snyder, Anne and Jerome Fisher Director; Carmela Teichman, Traveling Exhibitions Officer and Coordinator of Curatorial Services; and the other staff members of The Israel Museum, Jerusalem, who worked diligently with RAM's staff to realize this show. Finally, we at RAM are very happy to be working with Hudson Hills Press and hope that this is the beginning of a warm, ongoing relationship.

Women's Tales: Four Leading Israeli Jewelers is a landmark exhibition and publication for the field of contemporary jewelry as well as for both Israel and the United States. Co-organizing such an international project is a joyful reminder that creativity is alive and well throughout our world and that exchanges of visual art are one of the best ways to promote communication and understanding between its peoples.

Bruce W. Pepich, *Executive Director and Curator of Collections*
Racine Art Museum

Preface and Acknowledgments

Ideas for exhibitions come from a variety of sources. Although the beginning of modern jewelry emerged from a European-American axis, in their seminal study *The New Jewelry: Trends and Traditions*, first published in 1985, the noted art and design writers and professionals Peter Dormer and Ralph Turner noted that since then developments have been taking place in other parts of the world, including Canada, Australia, and Japan. In particular they drew attention to the fact that "Israel is producing jewelers of the stature of Esther Knobel," and suggested in the future any critical study of modern jewelry would have to include a wider group of countries. Their words have inspired this journey.

Begun approximately three years ago, this exhibition has been for one of us an occasion to reconnect with old colleagues; for the other, it has been an opportunity to study previously unknown international developments within a familiar art form. For both, it has been a chance to learn about similarities and diversity within international museums and, specifically in this case, between American and Israeli culture. The common ground has been the art, and we wish above all to thank the artists for their cooperation. Each one has contributed to making this project important and memorable. Their own passion for their work has infused the exhibition and accompanying book.

Many individuals have contributed to the success of this project. We first want to extend our warmest appreciation to Dale and Doug Anderson and Andrea and Charles Bronfman who made the collaboration between The Israel Museum, Jerusalem, and the Racine Art Museum a reality. We also thank the International Partnerships Among Museums program (IPAM), administered by the American Association of Museums (AAM) and funded by the Department of State's Bureau of Educational and Cultural Affairs (ECA), which facilitated the initial travel and research

for this project. Helen W. Drutt English deserves our deep thanks for her contribution to the publication. We want to thank Terry Ann R. Neff, who has guided us with patience and resolve through the conceptualization and preparation of this publication; her friendship and support are greatly valued. Michael Tropea should be thanked for his brilliant photography of the objects. Special thanks also go to Leslie van Breen of Hudson Hills Press for her commitment to this publication, and to Susan Evans of Design per se for her elegant presentation.

In addition, we thank the American venues whose participation in the exhibition underscores its timeliness. It has been a great privilege to work with Michael Monroe, Bellevue Arts Museum, Washington; Amanda Clifford, Houston Center for Contemporary Craft; and Ulysses Dietz, The Newark Museum, whose commitment will enable the exhibition to be seen from coast to coast.

On the RAM staff, the wonderful support and guidance of Executive Director Bruce W. Pepich has been very critical to this exhibition and book. The final stages of this project reflect the diligence and careful thought of David Zaleski. We would also like to thank R. Michael Nitsch for his ongoing care and commitment to this project. Personal thanks should also be extended to Deb Bellgraph, who has consistently provided advice and friendship during the organization of this show. The special efforts in realizing this exhibition by RAM's Museum Store staff must be noted; warmest thanks should be extended to Lisa Englander, Museum Store Manager, Lauren Bell, Cassandra Coley, Laura Grayson, Sarah Nielsen, and Patricia Roberson. In addition, Laura D'Amato, Sue Buhler-Maki, Brenda Kenth, Heather Pugh, James Sheppard, John Coley, Marc Wollman, Jessica Zalewski, and Laura Gillespie deserve mention for their invaluable contributions. Terri White from the Milwaukee

Art Museum, who assisted with conservation while the objects were at RAM, should also be commended for her willing assistance.

On the staff at IMJ, we would like to thank James S. Snyder, Anne and Jerome Fisher Director, for his full support of this project. We would also like to thank Suzanne Landau, Yulla and Jacques Lipchitz Chief Curator of the Arts; and Yigal Zalmona, Chief Curator-at-Large, for their invaluable input and advice. Associate Curator Osnat Sirkin and Assistant Curator Nirit Sharon-Debel have assisted with research and the development of the project. They have been a wonderful team. Anna Barber, Senior Editor of English Publications, and Navva Milliken assisted in the preparation of the manuscript drafted in Israel. Our very special thanks to Carmela Teichman, Traveling Exhibitions Officer and Coordinator of Curatorial Services, for her fine job as liaison between IMJ and RAM. Finally, we appreciate the professionalism of the various departments that assisted in this project: Eli Tzipi Goldschmidt from the Object Conservation Laboratory, and IMJ's Technical Services headed by Pesach Ruder, and Henk van Doornik from the Loan and Shipping Office.

Davira S. Taragin, *Director of Exhibitions and Programs*
Racine Art Museum

Alex Ward, *Curator of Design and Architecture*
The Israel Museum, Jerusalem

11

The Essays

Israeli Identity and Collective Memory

Alex Ward

The Historical Context

Athough it stands at the crossroads of Europe, Asia, and Africa, Israel is far removed from the cosmopolitan centers of the world. Consequently, its art has developed in an environment completely unlike that of Europe or America. In fact, the intensity and transitory condition of daily life so permeate the consciousness of Israel's people—and, by inclusion, her artists—that all artistic expression, however individualized, is in some measure deeply informed by the national context in which it has been created.

Whether obtained from stories told at home, at school, heard on the radio, or seen on television, every Israeli carries the collective baggage of Jewish history: from the destruction of the Second Temple, to two thousand years of exile, to pogroms, to the Holocaust, to the establishment of the state of Israel in 1948. The generation that grew up in the 1950s in Israel—through kindergarten, youth organizations, high school, and service in the Israel Defense Forces (IDF)—has also been brought up, through literature and songs, with the myths of fallen heroes accompanied by a strong connection to the land. These myths and iconic images have become an important component of Israeli identity and consciousness.

The history of the modern state of Israel begins with the early Zionist movement, whose primary goal was to encourage the "Return to Zion." A strategy for achieving this goal was through a program of education and literature. Field trips to the countryside were organized by schools, youth organizations, and the army. One result was the establishment of a deeply felt connection to the land—probably the strongest unifying element for many Israelis, including the four artists featured in this book.

From childhood to adulthood, Israelis have been brought up with war and images of soldiers, tanks, and airplanes. Their songs tell of war and peace. Their education includes tales of the invincibility and mythic image of the IDF and the story of the hero Joseph Trumpeldor, who with his dying breath during the battle of Tel Hai in 1920, whispered: "It is good to die for our country." The famous monument of a roaring lion erected near his grave is a national symbol of sacrifice and heroism (fig. 1).

During Israel's early years, there was a lot of indoctrination surrounded by ideology and local mythology. It was not until the 1980s, when historians were allowed to examine classified documents, that some of the myths of Zionism learned in schools were shattered. Through the end of the 1950s, the doctrine of the collective "We" had been embedded into the consciousness of every Israeli. It played a major role in uniting the country in its common struggle to survive all the hardships and battles against its hostile Arab neighbors. But as the decade drew to a close, the collective spirit was gradually being superseded by the spirit of the individual. Since its founding, the state of Israel has lived with contradictions produced by the tempestuous ideological, political, and moral disagreement within its own society; but it was the decade of the 1960s that saw the first dramatic indications of the country's future direction.

The 1960s saw political and cultural upheaval throughout the world, particularly in the United States, where a disenchanted new generation protested against discrimination, the Vietnam War, and the entrenched values of the establishment. Repercussions of this tide of rebellion and change were felt in Europe, but Israel's youth were to wait another decade before mobilizing.

Fig. 1 Trumpeldor memorial at Tel Hai with a member of the Hagana (clandestine Jewish defense force) standing guard, 1938
Photographer: Zoltan Kluger
Collection of the Israel National Photo Collection, Jerusalem
©Israel National Photo Collection, Jerusalem

14

One of the most dramatic events in the history of Israel during the 1960s was the 1967 Six-Day War; its implications still affect the country today. Following the war's unprecedented and victorious conclusion, the country tripled in size and was swept by a great wave of patriotism and a sense of invincibility. Nevertheless, in the midst of all this pride and celebration lurked a feeling that true peace was no closer than before, and that everyone was still just waiting for new hostilities to erupt. Uri Avnery, an Independence War veteran-turned-radical-peace-advocate, clearly set the tone against the tide of nationalism in the magazine *Ha Olam Ha Ze (This World)*, which during its existence in the 1950s and 1960s influenced the perceptions of two generations of Israeli youth.

The euphoria of the Six-Day War was dashed by the outbreak of the 1973 Yom Kippur War, an existential nightmare for Israel. Suddenly, economic boom turned into galloping inflation, adding salt to the wounds of those dejected and angered by the short-sightedness and arrogance of politicians and military commanders. The many anti-establishment protests led to the dramatic rise of the right-wing Likud Party in the elections of 1977, with long-term consequences. Later the same year, Egypt's President Anwar Sadat made a historic visit to Israel, and in 1979 the first peace treaty between Israel and an Arab nation was signed. Sadat's trip sparked a massive demonstration in Tel Aviv, opposing the establishment of settlements in the territories occupied since the 1967 war. This event marked the birth of "Peace Now," the first national political left-wing peace protest movement in Israel.

The first generation of the state of Israel, usually known as The State Generation *(Dor Ha Medina)*, had grown up along with the nation but were much more critical. Tired of the old patriotic slogans, they openly voiced their opinions. The generation that would come to maturity in the 1970s began to echo the zeitgest of the youth counter-culture in America. The accessibility of foreign radio stations informed this generation about events happening abroad and encouraged them to seek change in their own country. Predictably, it was the arrival of television in 1968 that had the greatest impact on Israeli society and its connection to the world.

The massive Israeli military incursion into Lebanon in the summer of 1982, called "Operation Peace for Galilee," brought large demonstrations by members of the left wing. Because they saw Israel as the invader, this was the first war that sharply divided the country. In 1983, Minister of Defense Ariel Sharon was forced to resign after an Israeli inquiry concluded that he had failed to act to prevent the massacre in the Sabra and Shatila refugee camps in September 1982.

Meanwhile, the process of modernization—and "Americanization"—of Israel was rapid. During the 1980s and 1990s, many Israelis began moving into suburban communities with their own shopping malls and health club facilities. As the 1990s progressed, more and more people spent their time in front of computers in air-conditioned offices or at home. Eventually, no one could be without a mobile phone or cable television. Today, almost everything is purchased by plastic, which began to take hold in Israel only in the late 1980s. Increasingly, Israelis found the power and freedom as consumers to choose their health plan, select their child's education, or book a holiday abroad.

The illusion of normalcy was shattered by Scuds landing in the suburbs of Tel Aviv during the Gulf War in 1991 and, again, during the campaign of indiscriminate terror and violence of the second Intifada in 2000. Buses being blown up by suicide bombers in Jerusalem and Tel Aviv suddenly made war and terrorism a personal experience for Israelis.

In September 1993, an overwhelming sense of optimism was awakened in Israel by the historic handshake under the eyes of United States President William Clinton on the White House lawn between Yitzhak Rabin, the Israeli Prime Minister, and his arch enemy, Yasser Arafat, Chairman of the Palestine Liberation Organization; a peace treaty with Jordan followed. The elation was dashed by one of the darkest moments in Israel's history, when Rabin was assassinated by an Israeli religious extremist during a peace demonstration on November 4, 1995, plunging the country into deep mourning. The collapse of the Oslo Accords reflected the radical shift to the right of a public skeptical about the peace process. The result was the election of Ariel Sharon as Prime Minister in 2001.

Fig. 2 Unknown designer
*Keren Hayesod Plants—The Jewish
People Harvest*, 1940s
Silkscreen
27 1/2 x 19 1/2 inches
Collection of The Israel Museum,
Jerusalem, Gift of Jacqueline
Frydman-Klugman, Paris
©The Israel Museum, Jerusalem,
Ofrit Rosenberg Ben-Menachem

Fig. 3 Unknown photographer
The silver department at the Bezalel
School of Arts and Crafts, Jerusalem,
1909
Collection of The Israel Museum,
Jerusalem
©The Israel Museum, Jerusalem

16

The history of Israel has been plagued by war and conflict with its Arab neighbors—a dismaying record of despair, mistrust, and hatred. It is an intractable conflict in which the Israelis and Palestinians have each laid claim to their historical rights. In the absence of any clear border or direction, the situation is constantly in flux with a peace settlement still only a hope, not a reality.

The Cultural Context

As with all Israelis, the land itself is the strongest common touchstone for some of the nation's artists, who often use landscape as a point of identification with their country. Posters depicting planting, growing, and blossoming have served as popular metaphors for national revival (fig. 2). The famous poet Shaul Tchernikovsky declared: "Man is nothing but the image of his native landscape."[1] In this spirit, traditional holidays have been reinterpreted in terms of the land's ancient roots and agricultural associations. The holiday of Shavuot (Pentecost), for example, is marked in the kibbutz by parades and great festivity; in the cities, kindergarten children dress in white, wear wreaths of flowers on their heads, and carry baskets filled with fruits symbolizing the offering of the first fruits in the Temple in ancient times. In the 2003 exhibition "Old-New Land: First Flowers of Israeli Art" at The Israel Museum, Jerusalem, curator

Tamar Manor-Friedman spoke of the works and approach to the world of flowers by a younger generation of Israeli artists as "a personal statement of their attempt to strike root in their physical and cultural surroundings."[2]

One of Israel's leading arts institutions has a history that considerably predates the founding of the state. Three of the artists in this exhibition, Vered Kaminski, Esther Knobel, and Deganit Stern Schocken, all studied at Bezalel Academy. Bezalel Academy of Art and Design, as it is now known, was founded in 1906 in Jerusalem as the Bezalel School of Arts and Crafts by the visionary figure Boris Schatz. With the mission of promoting Jewish handicraft work, the school embraced biblical subjects and an eclectic style— the "Bezalel Style"—which combined Western modes with Oriental arabesques and Damascus work (brass or copper decoratively inlaid with copper and silver). One of the first departments established by Schatz was the division of metalwork, where Yemenite artisans developed their crafts (fig. 3). Schatz eventually extended the techniques of the school to include brass casting, spinning, cutting, die-stamping, and gem polishing. The school closed in 1929 because of financial difficulties. It reopened in 1935 as "The New Bezalel."

The 1930s saw the arrival of many German-Jewish refugees fleeing the Nazi regime. These immigrants

1. S. Tchernikovsky, "Man is nothing but...," in *The Complete Writings of Shaul Tchernikovsky, Vol. A: Poems and Ballads* (Tel Aviv: Am Oved Publishers, 1990), p. 285.

2. Tamar Manor-Friedman, "First Flowers of Israeli Art," in *Old-New Land: From the Early Days of Israeli Art* (Jerusalem: The Israel Museum, Jerusalem, 2004), www.imj.org.il/eng/exhibitions/2003/old_new_land/first_flowers.html.

quickly dominated the art scene in Jerusalem and became strongly associated with the aims of The New Bezalel. The pedagogic direction of the school shifted radically, rejecting Orientalism in favor of Modernism and the tradition of the Bauhaus. Adhering to Bauhaus ideals, the school began to focus on bridging the gap between pure and practical art. In the mid-1960s, under the directorship of Professor Dan Hoffner, Bezalel again experienced a major renewal. In just fifteen years, it was transformed from an outdated school into the first Israeli art academy accredited to award bachelor's degrees in fine arts and design.

At this time, the art scene in Tel Aviv shifted its focus from French lyrical abstraction to American Pop. The collages of Robert Rauschenberg were especially influential, but the work of Larry Rivers and Jim Dine also captured the attention of young and emerging artists. In 1965, the radical arts group "Ten Plus" was formed in Tel Aviv by the artist Raffi Lavie. The organization chose unusual themes, held a group paintings exhibition, and arranged evening events with individuals from literature, music, and the theater. Writers such as Amos Oz, Aharon Appelfeld, and A. B. Yehoshua rebelled against the dominant collective spirit, and wrote about the condition of the individual and the family.

Immediately following the Yom Kippur War, from 1974 to 1976, Israel's art community felt a pressing need to focus on social issues and face political reality.[3] The country was deeply divided. Political radicalism swept the Bezalel Academy. Rebelling against drawing and painting, fine-arts students instigated anarchistic actions, strutting around wearing firing targets—an enactment of the concept "sniper artists"—and engaging in political performance art. The students in the jewelry department, however, chose to focus on their work rather than join in these political activities.

The achievements of Bianca Eshel-Gershuni, Vered Kaminski, Esther Knobel, and Deganit Stern Schocken are especially impressive given the lackluster history of contemporary jewelry in Israel. Although Bezalel's Department of Gold and Silversmithing has been recognized since the 1970s as Israel's leading department of its kind, many of its graduates did not engage in serious artistic careers, opting instead to produce

3. Gideaon Ofrat, *One Hundred Years of Art in Israel* (Boulder, Colorado: Westview Press, 1998). p. 307.

for the commercial jewelry market or to craft Jewish ritual objects, with some producing one-off pieces for group exhibitions. Eshel-Gershuni, Kaminski, Knobel, and Stern Schocken, however, have consistently created artistic jewelry that has gained international recognition.

The nation's lack of a strong artistic contemporary jewelry movement may have been due in part to the absence in either Jerusalem or Tel Aviv of an avant-garde jewelry gallery such as London's Electrum Gallery or Amsterdam's Gallery Ra. The radical contemporary jewelry movements that developed in Europe and the United States from the mid-1970s to the 1980s did not reach Israel. Unlike local ceramists, who formed an active coalition to represent their achievements, the jewelers today have still not united to create a unified artistic community. In fact, the first biennial for jewelry in Israel was initiated only in 1998, when it was curated by Bianca Eshel-Gershuni and Esther Knobel. The second jewelry biennial was curated by Vered Kaminski. Recently, the third one was curated by Deganit Stern Schocken.

In the absence of vanguard activity at home, their experiences abroad in Europe certainly opened the eyes of Kaminski, Knobel, and Stern Schocken. Beginning in the mid-1970s, a new movement in jewelry began to develop in Holland and England. Reacting against the preciousness and exclusivity of jewelry, its associations with wealth and status, and even its relationship to the human body, young avant-garde jewelers sought to dismantle traditional conventions. Seeking greater freedom to do more personal work, they advocated that the merit of a piece of jewelry should be judged not by the value of the materials but by the concept of the piece. They turned to industrial materials such as aluminum, stainless steel, and black rubber instead of gold and gemstones. They also found new ways to manufacture and color their works, such as anodizing aluminum, casting resin, and working in acrylic.

Two of the most influential figures of the New Jewelry movement in Europe were the Dutch jewelers Emmy van Leersum and Gijs Bakker. Beginning in the late 1960s, they extended the international debate about jewelry's role in society. Their innovative and radical experiments greatly influenced the new generation of jewelry students in England and elsewhere in the 1970s and 1980s.

Since the mid-1990s, the Department of Jewelry and Metalwork at the Bezalel Academy of Art and Design has gone through a radical change, and it is now called the Department of Jewelry, Accessories and Objects. The emphasis is now on the design of outfits, shoes, bags, hats, fashion, and performance accessories, to the gradual decline of the area of contemporary jewelry. In 1998, the Shenkar College of Engineering and Design, Ramat Gan, famous for its fashion and textile departments, opened a new Department of Jewelry Design. The direction of the department so far reflects a rather conservative approach to the area of industrial jewelry.

The Artists

The four jewelry artists featured here have individual histories that extend across varying backgrounds, locations, and personal memories. Over a period of more than thirty years, their collective artistic output has developed into maturity, but in very different ways. Unlike the refinement and precision of the works of Kaminski and Stern Schocken, the works of Eshel-Gershuni and Knobel have a much greater sense of physicality and sensuousness in the treatment of materials. They appear to be created out of a painterly attitude, which gives them a very different inner soul and presence. Surely these qualities are due in part to the influence of their teachers: Eshel-Gershuni studied under the highly acclaimed painters Yehezkel Streichman and Yosef Zaritsky, leading figures in the "New Horizons" group, active in Tel Aviv during the 1950s and devoted to French lyrical abstraction; Knobel studied under Raffi Lavie, the founder of "Ten Plus."

Yet, however unique and distinctive the work and resumé of each, these artists share the experience particular to their national identity. Eshel-Gershuni has imposed a strict daily studio regimen upon herself, which hints at the obsessive ritual of a religious ceremony. Similarly, Kaminski, Knobel, and Stern Schocken feel a magnetic force drawing them into an intimate and ritualistic world, secure and protected from the struggles and confrontations outside. All have taken inspiration from the "local" as well as the "personal." Following very singular journeys of self-discovery, they have made major contributions to the field of avant-garde jewelry in Israel.

An Outsider's Perspective: Life Stories

Davira S. Taragin

As an American curator specializing in American contemporary crafts, I am accustomed to seeing jewelry that emphasizes narrative. Moreover, as a woman educated during the emergence of the women's movement in America, I am particularly sensitive to women's issues as defined in America. It is perhaps this dual orientation that enabled me, when visiting the studios of Bianca Eshel-Gershuni, Vered Kaminski, Esther Knobel, and Deganit Stern Schocken in Israel, to discover—to my surprise—that all four artists express in their work autobiographical aspects of their lives as women, wives, and mothers. These artists have adopted the tenets of Europe's New Jewelry movement in their innovative use of materials and in the interaction of their jewelry with the body. Yet, in addition to this fundamental emphasis on form in relation to concept and function, they also make dramatic personal statements in their jewelry that, consciously or not, reflect issues frequently addressed by women artists.

Eshel-Gershuni, Kaminski, Knobel, and Stern Schocken are by no means blatant feminists, yet certain elements of their lives have marked those of women artists for centuries. In her historic study published in 1977, Ann Sutherland Harris noted that most women artists before the nineteenth century were often either married to or were the daughters of artists.[1] At some time in their lives, these Israeli jewelers also have been closely involved with men in the arts. For instance, Knobel's husband is Alex Ward, a painter and textile designer who is now the Curator of Design and Architecture at The Israel Museum, Jerusalem; Knobel feels that he has played a critical role in keeping her abreast of developments in contemporary art and design.

These four Israeli jewelers emerged during the late 1960s, 1970s, and early 1980s, respectively. During this period, in the early 1970s, there was an explosion of work internationally that reflected the insertion of women's autobiographical experiences into the practices of making art and a conscious acceptance of this content among some women artists. Reinforcing the legitimacy of this direction, the careers of earlier women artists such as Mexican Surrealist painter Frida Kahlo, who took a similar approach, were the subject of considerable scholarly reexamination, resulting in their being elevated to cult status. The work of Knobel and Eshel-Gershuni can be viewed within the context of this period.

I also see parallels between Knobel's interest in surface decoration in the late 1970s and 1980s and the larger Pattern and Decoration movement in the United States. Some feminist art historians consider this movement's concern with surface as part of a larger response against the traditional gender-based concept of the "decorative."[2] Conscious of this American movement since its inception, Knobel always has utilized surface decoration to express the conceptual.

In a similar vein, Stern Schocken's body pieces from the late 1980s and early 1990s embrace and protect the body in ways that recall the work of many video and performance artists of the 1970s, who used their bodies to make autobiographical statements.[3] Finally, the complex, laborious nature of traditional handicrafts done by women is present in the ways in which Kaminski and Eshel-Gershuni deal with process. While Eshel-Gershuni's work is about shaping and manipulating her surfaces, Kaminski's painstaking execution of each piece through bending, cutting, casting, and/or soldering evokes, for me, the interest during the mid-1960s and 1970s in the physical process of making art by sculptors such as Jackie Winsor and Lynda Benglis.

Of the four Israeli artists, Eshel-Gershuni and Stern Shocken are willing to draw comparisons between their own careers and those of other women artists.

1. For the groundbreaking study on this subject, see *Women Artists 1550–1950*, text by Ann Sutherland Harris and Linda Nochlin (Los Angeles County Museum of Art, 1976). Harris, as a professor of art history at Barnard College, first directed the present author to issues concerning women in art history.

2. For an excellent discussion of the role of women within late twentieth-century art, see Whitney Chadwick, *Women, Art, and Society* (London and New York: Thames and Hudson, Inc., 1990), pp. 296–335, passim.

3. The relationship between contemporary European jewelry and video and performance art of the 1970s is explained in detail in David Ward, "Work in the Collection: A Broader Context and Related Activities," in *The Jewellery Project: New Departures in British and European Work 1980–83* (London: Crafts Council Gallery, 1983), pp. 7–12.

Stern Schocken regularly cites the work of British installation artist Rachel Whiteread and German performance, installation, and video artist Rebecca Horn as critical to the development of her aesthetic. Similarly, she is very proud that her work has been compared to that of Deconstructivist architect Zaha Hadid.[4] Eshel-Gershuni draws very strong parallels between her own life and that of Kahlo, since both women were married to artists and suffered serious accidents. She is pleased that others have seen the relationship between her organic forms and those of sculptor Louise Bourgeois. She also strongly relates to the work of iconic British designer Vivienne Westwood, whose fashions address the meaning of dress, its cultural and historical precedents, and the emotional and physical effect it exerts on the wearer. Eshel-Gershuni compares her career to that of Westwood since they both came to their respective fields from fine arts backgrounds.

Kaminski and Knobel, on the other hand, reject having their work interpreted in terms of gender issues. Growing up on a kibbutz, Kaminski claims that she never experienced discrimination because of her sex. While recognizing that jewelry is generally designed to be feminine and made for women, she has always seen her own as "hardy" and unisex. She is proud that her brooches and stainless-steel bracelets are worn by both men and women.

Knobel, likewise, is adamant that "being a woman does not influence my work any more or less than the fact that I am a daughter, a sister, a mother, a wife, a friend… and so on."[5] In fact, an autobiographical interpretation of her work may even be controversial since Knobel sees her jewelry within the context of the New Jewelry movement and its concern with materials and the relationship with the body. She defines it as an "art that is to be borne and relates to human scale and memory." Nonetheless, of the artists in this exhibition, Knobel's work appears to me to be most explicitly about content,[6] and deals not only with everyday life but *her* everyday life. Her subject matter often references her immediate family, the experience of living in Jerusalem, and her memories of childhood. One of her better-known pieces is, in fact, about her family: *"The Prince" Handpiece* (EK cat. no. 16) is a proud mother's wearable rendition in tin of a photo-graph of her four-year-old son. Furthermore, as the daughter of Holocaust survivors and the mother of a single male child in a country continually at war, Knobel frequently has dealt with its threats and horrors. *Camouflage Necklace* (EK cat. no. 7), created in response to Israel's 1982 war with Lebanon, for instance, symbolizes the garlands for graves that, as a commodity of everyday life in Israel, can be purchased at any neighborhood florist.[7]

Nature is also a constant motif in Knobel's work, demonstrating the strong influence of the society in which she grew up. The artist recalls that the Israel of the 1950s was a poor country with few luxuries to purchase in its shops. Nurtured by "a good mother-daughter dialogue on aesthetical issues,"[8] Knobel looked to the countryside as a source of inspiration. One of the artist's earliest works, *Pine Tree Needles* (EK cat. no. 1), uses anodized aluminum to make a chain of loops shaped like pine needles, recalling the necklaces she made as a child from materials that she found in nature.

In telling the story of her days, Knobel has chosen to use mundane, often neglected materials, adding significantly to the New Jewelry movement's experimentation with materials. In 1980/81 she began using recycled tin cans, often from food products, cutting the metal into brooches with visible clasps (EK cat. no. 4b). The idea for this unprecedented body of work came from her daily walks along sidewalks littered with tin cans and debris. "I am an earthy person, finding inspiration by looking downwards towards the ground."[9] By the late 1980s and early 1990s, she was incorporating materials directly from nature, for example, a ball of raw cotton in *"Cotton" Scarf* (EK cat. no. 13) and then fruit and dried vegetables as decoration in a series of baskets intended to re-create childhood memories of the Jewish harvest celebration of Pentecost (EK cat. nos. 18, 19). By the mid-1990s, laminated flower petals had become an essential part of her vocabulary. Even when using precious materials, Knobel is intrigued by the properties of the discarded. For instance, *Dahlia Ring* (EK cat. no. 28), created during a residency at Penland School of Crafts in North Carolina, is made of scraps of silver.

20

4. Helen W. Drutt English and Peter Dormer, *Jewelry of Our Time* (New York: Rizzoli International Publications, 1995), p. 69.

5. Esther Knobel, e-mail to the author, August 1, 2005.

6. Contemporary literature published in conjunction with exhibitions of Knobel's work at Galerie Ra, Paul Derrez's highly respected gallery in Amsterdam, frequently focuses on her subject matter.

7. For a good discussion of the iconography of Knobel's work, see "Esther Knobel—Sketches in Raw Material," in *Esther Knobel* (Amsterdam: Galerie Ra, 1994).

8. Esther Knobel, e-mail to the author, November 1, 2005.

9. Esther Knobel in conversation with the author, November 1, 2005.

One of the first Israeli women artists to use her paintings, sculptures, and jewelry to convey her experiences as a woman,[10] Eshel-Gershuni denies any feminist associations although she sees herself as the antithesis of her homemaker mother. "I am not about fighting in the streets or throwing away my bra but I know my rights.... For a woman to create is harder than for a man. Caring for small kids and the house falls to the mother. I have been working all my life. It is very hard to balance career and children. The price that I pay for being a woman and a mother is not traveling all over the world and being famous."

Claiming that making art is "therapy," Eshel-Gershuni creates work that is about love and death—for her, the essence of life in Israel. Forced to immigrate to Palestine as a child in 1939, she found in art a means to vent her feelings of victimization that resulted from living in a war-torn country and a series of ill-fated relationships beginning with the death of her twenty-seven-year-old husband in the 1956 Sinai War. "I always feel like the victim," she says, "but like Jesus, I am a survivor." She draws direct parallels between her own sufferings and those of Jesus and envisions women as Christ figures.

Remembrances of love lost, the loneliness and difficulty of being a single parent, and surviving as an artist in an embattled land are the inspirations behind much of Eshel-Gershuni's jewelry, most of which was made for exhibitions or her own use and not the marketplace. *"My Grave," Ring* (BE-G cat. no. 13), for example, which alludes to the design of her own grave, is not intended to be morbid. On the contrary, it refers to the celebration that she imagines will occur in heaven when she meets the soul of her dead husband. She depicts her final resting place as inhabited by rabbits eating and enjoying life in the midst of death—a metaphor for the intense pleasure that Eshel-Gershuni finds in making her art despite life's challenges. Almost thirty-five years later, she responded similarly to the outbreak of the Gulf War in 1991 by creating a series of brooches (BE-G cat. nos. 21–24) whose imagery started as fish— a Christian symbol—and evolved into the fighter planes she saw on television.

It is scarcely a surprise, therefore, to learn that likenesses of turtles emerged as the subject of the last large body of jewelry that the artist created in the

1990s and her more recent paintings and sculptures. For Eshel-Gershuni, the "wonderful, mythological creature" is a personification of her being, its shell the "shelter for the self."[11] She draws parallels with its physical state and also the turtle's slow movements and her own frustration in executing her numerous ideas for artwork. She notes how her tendency in her early works toward leaving the manipulated gold surfaces gave way to using found objects after the mid-1970s. By using "readymades" of tiny toys and elements from Victorian jewelry that reflect her sensibilities, she can tell her story without "wasting" time learning new metalworking techniques.

While both Knobel and Eshel-Gershuni use recognizable imagery to relay their experiences, Stern Schocken and Kaminski make autobiographical statements through their explorations of form and process. Employing labor-intensive techniques that in one piece can involve bending multiple wires, casting, and/or cutting and soldering, Kaminski's work relates directly to both the concern with process of the 1970s and the traditional handicrafts done by women. Based upon her thorough knowledge of the materials and techniques of goldsmithing,[12] her art is abstract, even Constructivist, in nature. Nevertheless, Kaminski insists that it closely reflects events in her life.[13]

Kaminski traces her aesthetic, in part, to the three years she spent in the late 1980s as a young mother working on her master's degree at the University of Paris VIII, Vincennes–Saint-Denis. Watching her son play in an enclosed area, she became fascinated with the design and texture of the fence, leading to a study of the patterns of fences, gates, and iron bars as part of her thesis. Back in Jerusalem by the early 1990s, she again looked to her physical environment for inspiration, in this case, to the walls along the highways that are made of giant wire screens that retain massed stones. The resulting series of bowls, necklaces, and brooches celebrate the native Jerusalem stone (VK cat. nos. 5, 6, 8–11, 13). Kaminski notes, "One basic purpose of jewelry, historically, is to hold precious stones that are set in metal. In my work, I use simple Jerusalem stones. They are precious to me because Jerusalem is my home, my city." When this work was first exhibited in 1991, Izzika Gaon, the late Curator of Design at The Israel Museum, Jerusalem, saw it as the artist's response to the first Intifada,

21

10. Sorin Heller, "Chapters in Personal Mythology," in *Bianca Eshel-Gershuni: Step by Step* (Tel Aviv Museum of Art, 2001), p. 67.

11. For a discussion of the image of turtles in Eshel-Gershuni's work, see Mordechai Gelman, "The Turtle of Innerness," in ibid., pp. 72–77.

12. For a good discussion of Kaminski's work, see Renate Menzi, "Der Schattenwurf einer Schale als Brosche," *Israelitisches Wochenblatt* 46 (November 14, 1997), pp. 24–26.

13. In the summer of 2002, Kaminski curated the Eretz Israel Museum's second biennial contemporary jewelry exhibition entitled "Chain Reaction: Israeli Jewelry 2." Unlike the first biennial, curated by Knobel and Eshel-Gershuni, which focused on contemporary jewelry as body adornment, Kaminski invited approximately fifty Israeli jewelers, designers, and artists to create pieces with specific messages about everyday life.

noting that Kaminski's stones and metal reference the rain of stones hitting automobile windshields protected with heavy iron grating.[14] Kaminski, however, is adamant that her work is not a statement about the political situation in Israel. "I feel good in Israel," she states. "While I see the Arab uprising, the Intifada, on TV, I do not feel it directly. People I am in contact with here are very nice and I have my work." Later bodies of work attest to this connection to place. For instance, the arrangement of stones on the hillside terraces that surround Jerusalem inspired *Bowl* (VK cat. no. 17) and a group of brooches constructed by soldering modified cast elements (VK cat. nos. 18, 21, 22, 24). Similarly, living in a Jerusalem made up of side-by-side Jewish/Arab neighborhoods has nurtured Kaminski's appreciation of Israel's multiculturalism. *Necklace* (VK cat. no. 25), for example, is reminiscent of an Islamic devotional object. Within the past few years, her exploration of the tree form as seen in the Israel Museum's sculpture 2^9 (VK cat. no. 23), and, more recently, in her $2^6 x 2$ *Earrings* (VK cat. no. 28), have paralleled her current involvement in the construction of a three-dimensional family tree. Trees also play a vital role in making Israel's arid soil fertile.

For Deganit Stern Schocken, form is a metaphor for personal expression. Her earliest brooches and necklaces demonstrate a rationalist approach to these objects, transforming typically insignificant functional elements such as clasps, hinges, spikes, and fabric into the focal points of her compositions. Later works examine the use of stones and the meaning of settings. Her most recent major body of work, titled *How Many Is One,* scrutinizes the entire industrial jewelry production process, providing new perspectives on less well-known stages of the process. The unifying theme behind all her work is a concern with construction and utilization of space, which reflects the influence of Whiteread's work but, more importantly, Stern Schocken's lifelong passion and involvement in architecture:

> I came to making jewellery…via architecture. I treat brooches by themselves as isolated signs, like buildings, like buildings whose significance can only be understood in terms of their dimensions and their relationship to their surroundings.

Single units placed on continuous lines create dynamic possibilities. Like streets, they form a network, a system of signs—*the city*! Jewellery is spread on the body, its earth—terra firma….[15]

On one level, the artist's approach to jewelry-making can perhaps be equated with her search for her own identity. Growing up on a kibbutz had a profound impact on the artist, both in increasing her awareness of the landscape and topography and in recognizing the importance of self. It encouraged Stern Schocken to be cognizant of the larger women's movement: "I think that the issue of ego is very important [and is] the basis of some significant element in [my] work…. The idea of the kibbutz was that everybody is the same, you work as much as you can and you get what you need. So women were equally entitled to fight for their own identity."[16] Initially trained in architecture at Jerusalem's Bezalel Academy of Art and Design, Stern Schocken worked for a brief time in Moshe Safdie's office. However, when her husband selected architecture as a career, Stern Schocken felt the need to find her own profession. The prospect of making jewelry, which took less time to realize than architectural commissions, appealed to the artist. However, her multiyear marriage and resulting relationship with Israel's prestigious Schocken family—major patrons of the early Modernist German architect Erich Mendelsohn—put Stern Schocken in a world dominated by modern architecture. Although she is conversant in the European New Jewelry movement and in American Studio Jewelry, her primary influence remains architecture and she returns to it often for inspiration.[17]

The evolution of Stern Schocken's aesthetic demonstrates her expanding awareness of recent developments in America, where jewelry is conceived not as body adornment but as sculpture.[18] American jewelers of both sexes, such as J. Fred Woell, Ramona Solberg, and Laurie Hall, who have worked in a narrative vein, often have made conceptual statements about their country's culture. Stern Schocken's work provides an interesting commentary on attitudinal changes regarding the role of women and the discovery of her own independence as a mature woman.[19] The early brooches and neckpieces demonstrate her emerging ambivalence toward jewelry's traditional sexual

22

14. Izzika Gaon, "Special Exhibit: Palevsky Design Pavilion," March 1991, in Vered Kaminski's personal archives.

15. Deganit Stern Schocken, "Body and Sign: Urban Jewelry," unpublished manuscript, 1999–2000 (?), in Deganit Stern Schocken's personal archives.

16. Deganit Stern Schocken, e-mail to the author, October 17, 2005.

17. For example, her participation in an architectural conference in Israel on the use of materials led to her investigation of stones and settings.

18. Stern Schocken has traveled and exhibited regularly in the United States.

19. For an interesting but unempirical article on the role of women in the Middle East, see Nechemia Meyers, "Israeli Women Grapple with Careers, Kids—Sexism," *The Jewish News Weekly of Northern California,* October 29, 1999.

connotations. She recently noted, "In all my objects, the body exists but very abstractedly. It could be there but doesn't have to be." When viewed off the body, these objects appear as sculpture. When worn on the chest, the brooches dialogue with the fabric of the surrounding clothing, focusing attention on that part of the body; similarly, her neck and body pieces encircle and caress the "landscape" of the body. The later works, however, such as *Two Pools (Not Brooches)* (DSS cat. no. 17), which have been compared to Tel Aviv buildings by Bauhaus-trained architects,[20] or recent projects such as *How Many Is One* (DSS cat. nos. 29–31),[21] were not designed to interact with the body and consequently contain no specific references to jewelry as sexual enhancement.[22] In fact, Stern Schocken now equates a woman's independence with the jewelry that she wears: "If a woman is really free, she doesn't need jewelry. It hides her."

Interestingly, unlike many American jewelers who see themselves as sculptors, all four of these artists define their roles narrowly within contemporary art and jewelry. Knobel and Kaminski primarily see their work within the revolution that led to the New Jewelry movement in Europe. Eshel-Gershuni modestly compares her jewelry to American metalwork of the period, and disclaims her work in comparison. Even Stern Schocken's periodic written assessments of her own art are always framed in terms of the history of jewelry and its traditional relation to the body.

Nevertheless, knowingly or not, these artists share an interest in the autobiographical that situates their oeuvre within the context of the larger, global concern with identity and self-revelation that pervades much of the art of the late twentieth and early twenty-first centuries, especially that of women. But, more significantly, as colleagues emerging in Israel within a single generation of women jewelers in the 1960s–80s, their statements about women's issues unite them in an intriguing new way. Like that of their counterparts in America who use jewelry to comment on one aspect of their society, the work of these four artists goes beyond New Jewelry's concern with technique and form and its relationship to the body to make note-worthy statements about the lives of women in Middle Eastern culture.

Author's Note: This essay was based upon a series of interviews by the author that took place in June 2004 and June 2005. The author would like to thank the four artists, Bianca Eshel-Gershuni, Vered Kaminski, Esther Knobel, and Deganit Stern Schocken, and also Aviva Ben-Sira, Laura Parke Amundson, Suzy Kirschner, Bruce W. Pepich, and Rivka Saker for their assistance in the preparation of this essay.

20. Rachel Sukman, "An Architecture of Little Things," in *Deganit Stern Schocken* (Tel Aviv: Office in Tel Aviv, 1995), [pp. 5–6]; *Tel Aviv in the Tracks of the Bauhaus* (Tel Aviv: Office in Tel Aviv, 1994).

21. When initially installed at the Tel Aviv Museum of Art, the individual elements of this piece were placed on a circular moving conveyor belt that visitors could walk around.

22. Itzhak Carmel, "Negative Work," in *How Many Is One: Deganit Stern Schocken* (Tel Aviv Museum of Art, 2003), pp. 58–67.

Three Days, Six Women, Four Tales

Helen W. Drutt English

Every man has reminiscences which he would not tell to everyone, but only to his friends. He has other matters in his mind which he would not reveal even to his friends, but only to himself, and that is secret....

—Fyodor Dostoyevsky, *Notes from the Underground*

Prologue

The memory of a journey, the history of things, reunites objects of art, ideas, and people. The filmmaker Luis Buñuel wrote in his autobiography that life without memory is no life at all. The memories of a three-day journey to Israel are part of a not-too-distant past. In June 2005, Davira S. Taragin and I embarked on a trip in search of women's tales, augmented by visiting studios, conducting oral histories, and brief stops at museums, with no time for traditional sightseeing. We were crossing the magical thresholds of the four artists whose lives we were recording; in a sense, we were telling their stories.

The Pulitzer Prize–winning scholar Leon Edel writes that biographical data is like an opera—reportage, gossip, massed archives, tape recorders—and from this emerges storytelling: tales.[1] The facts are not invented, but the form is fashioned by the observer. So, I begin.

June 6, 2005: Vered Kaminski, Jerusalem

Davira and I have just found each other in the David Ben-Gurion Airport near Tel Aviv. We are embarking on a journey of discovery and renewing friendships. Observing the crowded streets, we realize we have arrived on a historic day: it is Jerusalem Day, celebrating the unification of Jerusalem, an event related to the 1967 Six-Day War, and the noise level is high. Our taxi stands paralyzed by the other cars amidst billowing blue-and-white flags held high by the Israelis. Thirty-eight years, and yet there is still fighting and unrest. June 6, I remember, is also the anniversary of D-Day, when the Allied Forces landed in Normandy in 1944. The events are joined in my memory.

We approach our hotel in Jerusalem, a homogeneous architectural structure appropriate to any modern city. Davira points out the YMCA built in 1933 by Q. L. Harmon, who designed the Empire State Building in New York. This is the second major architectural site I have encountered on my first return to Israel since 1983. The first was the Ben-Gurion Airport designed by Skidmore, Owings & Merrill with Moshe Safdie. It was a surprise. I felt as if I had entered the Temple of Dendur: broad marble walls, grand illusions of unlimited space. Was this the new Israel?

It is evening. We have arrived at the home and studio of Vered Kaminski. The dust has settled down and there is a calmness in the city. Vered's home is one of several apartments created from a former Arab villa— one of the Arab structures in Jerusalem that were bought, not confiscated. As we enter through a low arch on the side of the building, the interior looks as if it is composed of poured concrete. Apart from the fabricated *Stacking Stools* (VK cat. no. 27), no work is visible at first. We look for signs of her studio, which is located within a low alcove. Snacks on a table are awaiting us, her guests. Her computer is ready to show us images. How the world has changed!

1. Marc Pachter, ed., *Telling Lives, The Biographer's Art* (Philadelphia: University of Pennsylvania Press, 1981).

24

Despite the sterility of the absence of visible work, Vered's quiet presence exudes a restrained confidence. She relates that she was born Vered Rozebruch in Kibbutz Revadim in 1953, the only child of her birth parents but part of a family of seven boys and seven girls who lived together in the kibbutz. Like many others, she is a first-generation Israeli of Polish descent; her parents emigrated in 1950 (her mother died just last week), but most of her family perished during the Second World War. Women's tales: what do we really know of women's tales?

Vered lived in a children's house on the kibbutz. She visited her parents every day from four to seven pm, and during those hours she often occupied herself by making things, generally objects and jewelry. Her world expanded when she entered the army and again during her student years at the Bezalel Academy of Art and Design. At Bezalel, with such tutors as Arie Ofir, Amitai Kav, Yisrael Dahan, and Benny Bronstein, her education flourished; she also came in contact with visiting faculty such as Claus Bury, and later, after graduation, Gijs Bakker and Emmy van Leersum. Travels in Europe, residencies in Paris and Amsterdam, and studies with Onno Boekhoudt at the Rietveld Academy in 1979–80 followed. Her aesthetic was shaped by the prevalent attitudes of the Bauhaus; her love of jewelry continued and has always been central to her development as an artist. In 1992, she stated: "My works are mostly based on ancient principles of the roles of jewelry—I lean on this tradition while creating new pieces."[2]

Vered brings some works to the table as well as a sketchbook that has meticulous drawings and studies for future projects. Precise drawings of circular links carefully spaced on the page form motifs reminiscent of magnified snowflakes. Small, carefully assembled metal constructions appear as miniature geometric sculptures awaiting final resolution: will they be for the body or enlarged for a public space or functional use?

Vered's jewelry has a diverse range. A brooch from 1991 consists of nuggets that rest in twisted nickel silver and form a sunburst of color (VK cat. no. 9); one wonders if the interest in the bijou nuggets comes from her residency in Paris. Stones are trapped in a continuous cage of gold that forms a necklace (VK cat. no. 11). Brooches with stones dangle in a constructed void (VK cat. no. 10), or rest inside a strong nickel silver and copper coiled lattice (VK cat. no. 5).

In Paris, where Vered earned a master's degree from the University of Paris VIII, Vincennes–Saint-Denis, she spent considerable time analyzing the construction as well as the aesthetic properties of gates, fences, and other ornamental forms used as barricades; the influence of twisted metal and its joinery is evident in some of her works. Vered commented that the work done in Israel took a less fine form than the more delicate Paris pieces. One brooch, a linear entanglement (VK cat. no. 13), resembles a Jackson Pollock or a cursive, stream-of-consciousness painting by Cy Twombly. Arcs, circles, and grids reminiscent of Sol LeWitt's studies from 1972—"arcs from one corner," "arcs from four corners," "arcs from two adjacent sides," "grids from one corner,"[3] are reminiscent in her work. These linear compositions, published by the Kunsthalle Bern, have reappeared in Vered's metalworks and pay homage to LeWitt's investigations. Her beautiful constructions form brooches, bracelets, and baskets rooted in mathematical ideas; familiar patterns take on a new life.

Vered begins her work in a formal manner, with a didactic point of view, and likes to use any material—glass, stone, metal. There were times she gathered stones from the streets of Jerusalem, giving them increased meaning because she incorporated them into her jewelry. Her concern for function has less to do with the mechanics of wearing than with a concept: "ART" takes its place in a room or a public space and jewelry takes its place on the body; it is to be worn. Her dedicated sense of precision and use of alternative materials are illustrated in her concrete brooches of 1992 (VK cat. no. 15). Brass, silver, stainless steel, and copper patterns are connected in intricately cut shapes that join once more to form baskets and several series of brooches (VK cat. nos. 17, 18, 21, 22). From these mosaiclike works of 1996–98, we are unexpectedly confronted with a body of delicate filigree bracelets and sculpture (VK cat. nos. 23, 26).

2. *IIIème Triennale du Bijou* (Paris: Musée des Arts Décoratifs, 1992), p. 52.

3. Sol LeWitt, *Arcs, Circles & Grids* (Bern: Kunsthalle Bern and Paul Bianchini, 1972).

25

The diversity of Vered's work compliments the quiet and unassuming personality of the artist. Friends suddenly arrive, our working visit ends, and we are swept into a dark Jerusalem and a local café.

June 7, 2005: Esther Knobel, Jerusalem

There are many facets to the modern city of Jerusalem, a city that rose new from the ground. From the awesome wall of the old city with its fringelike border of tourist buses, to great vistas in an endless beyond punctuated with an occasional dome of gold, to slopes covered with cemeteries, everything is cohesively brought together under a carpet of Jerusalem stone.

This morning, Davira and I, laden with luggage, arrive via taxi at 39 Bezalel, the home and studio of Esther Knobel. On this narrow, busy urban street, cars are close to the curb and there is no space for parking. A stone wall, with an occasional opening for entry, separates the inclined pavement from the street. Bearing our bags like human camels, we ring the bell at a cast-iron gate. Esther appears in art-world black.

The home of Esther Knobel and Alex Ward is tucked under the garden staircase on a lower level. We immediately sit at the kitchen table. It is as if no time has been erased. We are all talking at once. We settle down to coffee and learn that Esther was born in 1949 in Bielawa, Silesia, in the south of Poland, and immigrated with her parents a year and a half later to Ramat Hasharon, a suburb of Tel Aviv. She relates that at the funeral of Vered Kaminski's mother last week, Vered's father revealed that he knew that her parents were, like himself and his wife, also from Bielawa. It is amazing how the pull to know your birthplace is so strong—"even if it is an ugly, horrible birthplace[4]—she wrote in her correspondence with the German artist Wilhelm Mattar. Now she talks about doing archaeological excavations; for Esther, this is a metaphor for trying to find what is buried in her past; she seems to be looking for knowledge in the territory of feelings.

Esther enjoyed a healthy childhood and a good education; she was a member of the youth movement, which pressed Israeli identity. She was introduced to art in high school by a well-known Israeli artist, Raffi

Lavie, who was her teacher and became a sort of guru. Her father was a craftsman and sewed shoe tops and her mother was a creative thinker who led her into making use of her hands. An early interest in architecture waned because she was not drawn to math and physics. Instead, she brought her interdisciplinary interests to the Bezalel Academy's jewelry department. She liked the freedom of jewelry and the option of having some kind of skills that could lead to an open proposal; she enjoyed the training. Her mentor was Arje Griest, a well-known Danish artist who chaired the Department of Gold and Silversmithing at Bezalel until 1972.[5]

Esther's curiosity is unlimited. She explored painting, enamel work, and ceramics at the Europees Keramisch Werkcentrum in 's-Hertogenbosch, The Netherlands. In the late 1990s, she went to Hamar, Norway, to participate in a workshop with Gijs Bakker and Onno Boekhoudt. Large-scale works evolved from the project, but most important was the opportunity to work with others and to gain experience in new and expanded territory. As early as 1987, the technical aspect of her work was based upon changes of orientation. From the 1970s onward, she has explored the fabrication and color possibilities of metals such as aluminum, titanium, tin, copper, silver, and gold. She appreciates the solutions of simple, low-tech construction and views construction, color, and relationship to the body as important aspects of her work.[6]

Esther's work does not always immediately reveal the spontaneity of its creation; the pieces develop and take their shape as she sits at the bench. She is what she observes, whether it comes through reading, walking through the city streets, experimenting with other materials such as clay, or challenging herself with projects and thoughts distant from the concept of ornament. From 1977 to the present, she has explored an innovative range of ideas. Single aluminum loops join to form a continuous chain in 1977 and become entangled into a mass not unlike an Alan Saret sculpture (EK cat. no. 1). Diverse pieces of jewelry made from assorted tin cans take the form of a series of narrative works. Warriors, necklaces reminiscent of camouflaged fatigues, immigrants crowded in a boat (EK cat. nos. 4b, 5–9, 23, 24)—all attest to selected elements of Esther's personal past and references to

4. Esther Knobel, *Untitled Dialogue* (Legnica, Poland: The Gallery of Art in Legnica, 2003), p. 11.

5. Arie Ofir succeeded him and continued supporting international influences.

6. Interview with Esther Knobel, Jerusalem, June 7, 2005.

biblical history. For example, the warrior reminds one of Bar Kochba with his bow and arrow, prepared to defend himself against the Romans during the second-century revolt.

In 1994, romance enters as the image of a bride is repeated in a silver silhouette with a border of rose petals (EK cat. no. 26). A carpet of copper "jasmine" flowers continues her interest in floral design and a more delicate aesthetic (EK cat. no. 27). The metal stem holding a rosebud has become a signature work for Esther. This creativity has crossed over into the twenty-first century. A conceptual work entitled *My Grandmother Is Knitting Too* (EK cat. no. 30) displays the disparate, separate elements—thimble, pliers, spool of copper, enamel—that reflect Esther's agile mind, fertile experimentation, and the merger of her personal experience with her aesthetic investigation. She is a traveler—deep within herself she explores *her* world and *the* world with a spirit of adventure that brings to her audience creative evidence of a searching mind.

June 7, 2005: Deganit Stern Schocken, Herzelia

When Davira and I arrive via taxi at Deganit Stern Schocken's home in the Tel Aviv suburb Herzelia, images of Deganit's home in Baka, Jerusalem, briefly came to mind; in particular, I remembered the great olive tree in the courtyard and a green neighborhood reminiscent of the Berlin woods. We have become very independent, Davira and I—no requested rides, and independent travel via taxi. I recall the journey that Emily Kimbrough and Cornelia Otis Skinner made over three-quarters of a century ago in their legendary account of their trip to Europe, *Our Hearts Were Young and Gay*. Both Davira's heart and mine are a bit older than theirs and filled with a mission to gather the tales of four Israeli artists, rather than the anticipation that accompanies an inaugural European tour. The lexicon has also dramatically changed the meaning of gay in the past half-century.

Sholom Aleichem is a suburban street that might exist in countless neighborhoods in America, Australia, or England: late twentieth-century single-family dwellings sit on three-quarter–acre plots of land. Deganit greets us and explains that this became the home of her parents when she was twenty-one. Both are now dead. Like Vered, Deganit was born on a kibbutz, Kibbutz Amir, in 1947. Her father came from Cologne, Germany, and her mother from a small village in Lithuania; they emigrated in 1933 and 1936, respectively, as did Vered's parents at a later time. Evidence of Deganit's life before marriage is here. There is a Gan Ha Ha-Yot, a garden of animal sculpture created by her mother. The fused-metal constructions, which form a lattice, may have been an unconscious influence. Some years ago, Deganit moved to where her "youth" resided and subsequently established a home and studio.

Trying to reconcile this environment with her work is strange. My introduction to Deganit's multifaceted constructions occurred almost twenty years ago. Combinations of silver, gold, and carved porcelain moved on suspensions of metal cords; they took their place on the body in many ways; both the wearer and the artist could determine the placement. An architectural instinct combined with a sense of playfulness gave birth to the ideas. The works spanning the years 1981 to 2003 begin with intricate constructions in which the fastening element is an integral part of the brooch (DSS cat. no. 2). Planes of geometric metal are juxtaposed with rubber extensions (DSS cat. no. 1); threads of silver unite elements that have been fabricated (DSS cat. no. 5); some are pierced (DSS cat. no. 4). Nothing like this had been seen before— a curved organic shape of porcelain serves as a perch for a pearl. These works were exhibited in my eponymous gallery in Philadelphia and New York as well as at Bertha Urdang's gallery, New York, in the 1980s and 1990s, and they had an important influence on American work.

Deganit is an inventor of new forms, new mechanisms, new connecting links—idiosyncratic works that function as jewelry. Reminiscent of Rube Goldberg's cartoons of improbable situations, these works in metal are improbable ornaments that become probable when worn. Deganit's jewelry continues to explore esoteric realms. Unexpected formal coils of fabric

27

nestle within a silver structure (DSS cat. nos. 11, 12); this unanticipated combination of materials offers a richness that rivals the use of gems. The uniqueness and the original stake their claim.

Her form of expression has borne aspects of architecture. During her marriage to Hillel Schocken, an architect, her studio was situated within the environment of his practice. The structural dynamics were shared, although the scale of work obviously differed. One influential notion derived from architectural thinking was envisioning ships as houses. Walter Gropius, in particular, also saw the house as a sculpture that possessed a sense of mobility. Deganit was inspired by this concept in creating her *Pools* (DSS cat. nos. 17, 20, 21). She thought about ships, houses, floating water, man. If a ship could be a house, then water could be a stone. "From the idea that it might be possible to make a stone, instead of receiving one as a given, came the thought that one could perhaps make a stone out of any material, cloth, for example, or water. In the world of jewelry, the stone is a status symbol, a value which is positioned in the center, inside a house. When the stone is hard, like a diamond, we are occupied with stone. When the stone is liquid, we are occupied with the structure. In *Pools,* the structure or the house becomes the main thing—and the 'stone,' which is water, becomes an experience, not a material."[7]

Movement is very important in Deganit's work—her mechanisms invite us to experiment with the placement of a coil or the angle of a hinge. But movement has been a part of her life since childhood. Her mother taught movement without music—a concept that has been transferred to Deganit's work: metaphorically frozen in metals with the possibility of being engaged through mechanical innovations. In the IIIème Triennale du Bijou held in Paris in 1992, she stated that "The central theme is tension… we entertain the possibility of difference: absence."[8] The concepts evolved through a series of projects, beginning in the early 1990s with metaphorical landscape brooches that utilize thread and stone and in combination with silver, to define territories (DSS cat. nos. 23–25). Cookie-cutter shapes appeared in brooches (DSS cat. no. 26). In the same year, works on paper combine photocopied images with lines of thread and silver to create tension in two dimensions (DSS cat. no. 22). In her 2003–2004 project *How Many Is One,* Deganit confronted the concept of mass production by endowing normally discarded fragments with a sense of preciousness (DSS cat. nos. 29–31). Such demanding intellectual pursuits challenge the concept of ornament and jewelry with a profound inquiry and contemplation.

Deganit has made supper and we are joined by one of her friends, who is a publisher. We continue our discussions on literature, music, art, and politics until two o'clock in the morning.

June 8, 2005: Bianca Eshel-Gershuni, Ra'Anana

My first encounter with Bianca Eshel-Gershuni occurred twenty-two years ago. She was a very different woman at that time. Obsessed with the disillusion that comes when the unexpected enters your life and dominates your work, she lives in the same environment dominated by symbols of her painful experience. They had taken their place in her art and filled her first-floor studio. I think back to that first visit to Bianca's with Esther Knobel in 1983; even then, her first-floor studio space was consumed with the visible energy of her life and art. Today, one enters her life through the debris of a long-forgotten garden.

From the moment we meet Bianca, the strength of her persona is with us. We are embraced by an Israeli Brunhilde. We climb a rusted staircase to a second-floor home which now also contains her studio. There is no space available. The abundance of her existence is everywhere, and it resounds with the same depth as her amazing voice; memories, relics, and inspiration come together in sculpture, drawings, collages, dioramas, jewelry. Everywhere is the evidence of a constant work ethic and obsession with her creative forces, filled with narrative illusions to her life, symbols that have affected her, animals she loves. "I learn from the turtles. The turtles always swim alone, cross the ocean and lay their eggs, and return to their birthplace. They are lonely but heroic, don't lose energy, don't waste their energy."[9]

7. Rachel Sukman, *Deganit Stern Schocken* (Tel Aviv: Office in Tel Aviv, 1995).

8. *IIIème Triennale du Bijou* p.85.

9. Interview with Bianca Eshel-Gershuni, Ra'Anana, Israel, June 8, 2005.

It may seem strange that Bianca Eshel-Gershuni coincides historically with Esther Knobel, Deganit Stern Schocken, and Vered Kaminski, four women whose tales are linked historically through their European roots but certainly not their diverse styles. What brought Bianca to Israel? Warned by a friend that her father was on Germany's blacklist, in 1939 the family escaped from Sofia, Bulgaria, where Bianca Moskona had been born in 1932. Her father, Leon Moskona, was a textile engineer. Through his profession, he had made important contacts in Israel, and the family moved into one of the great Bauhaus residences in Tel Aviv. Leon Moskona built the Elmo factory, well-known for refining wool. Bianca developed her love of working from his example; from her mother, her visible pleasure in making a comfortable home. Expressing her passion for art in painting and sculpture, she moved toward embracing small objects and jewelry because she loved adorning herself.

The tragic death of Bianca's first husband in 1956 was shattering. She sought solace in making art. First came ceramics, which she studied with Shelly Harari in 1958, however, when she saw the metal and fire and the material running with heat, she felt something, and the romance with jewelry began.

Unlike for Esther, Deganit, and Vered, Bianca's life and work are an assemblage and an encounter. We have entered the world of Bianca, known to her teachers as "Levanna" for more than twenty years. Her environment is distinctive—fertile and unconventional. A series of sculptures surrounds the surfaces of the tables, which are covered with work. There is no place for a tape recorder or legal pad. Smells from the kitchen are pungent and begin to invade our senses. Here, the line between art and life has been erased. Bianca creates because she is. The ambience surrounding her is dense with creativity and living. The power of her work lies in its intense proximity to her existence; she works, reads, cooks, sleeps, dreams, and entertains her grandchildren all within the second floor of her house-studio in Ra'Anana.

Seen against the works of Esther, Deganit, and Vered, Bianca is a maverick. Some of the sculptures have a disturbing quality—an almost intentionally expressive protest against Minimalism. Her visual allegories

transport us into chthonic realms. Here, in her world, in this apartment, we are in the underworld, relieved only by Bianca's intense and passionate love of life. As we walk through assemblages situated in front of bookcases and pass drawings by artist friends, we realize that all dialogue occurs at the table over coffee or a meal. Suddenly, boxes with jewelry appear. Each brooch that she wears carries its own tale—the history of its birth or the episode in which it was worn or the individual to whom it invited a response.

"I am not making jewelry for exhibition. I'm doing it because I am in love with jewelry, not doing it to express myself. It is not how I express myself in my art. [Curator] Yona Fischer said, 'You are making small sculpture.' I said, 'I am making *big* jewelry—in harmony with the hand and body.'"[10]

Bianca's work comes from her imagination—in the true spirit of André Breton's Surrealist manifesto, which defended the imagination and "its right to create and explore the very limits of madness."[11] From dust, she develops forms that look like Baroque treasures with idiosyncratic elements. Assemblages of found objects create unctuous brooches, rings, and earrings; the titles expand the lexicon and lead you into the depths of Bianca's mind.

A sweep of feathers hangs like the tail of a horse and is caught by a red coral rose; it is combined with beaten gold and pearls (BE-G cat. no. 10)—and signals, once more, the ability of Bianca to take common materials and transform them into something unique to her personal oeuvre. The fetish quality is repeated in *Earring* (BE-G cat. no. 17) as feathers once more extravagantly celebrate and expand the concept of an ordinary work. The result is works of art that can only come from an original voice. Bianca's passion for everything fills the room. "If I had a mountain of gold, I would make a life's work—all of the house would be filled with gold."[12] Often, her mentor is an ancient animal: the turtle. Its image in her work can be traced to the Gulf War in 1991 (BE-G cat. nos. 21–24). When the war began, she created brooches that began as fish and evolved into airplanes. Frightened by this unanticipated mystical experience, she began reading about turtles and felt that their nature epitomized her feelings. Several works take their form from this creature.

10. Ibid.

11. Gerard Durozoi, *History of the Surrealist Movement* (Chicago: University of Chicago Press, 2002), p. 67.

12. Interview with Bianca Eshel-Gershuni.

29

A wall piece entitled *"Once There Was a Blue Turtle and My Mother Kept Silent Like a Turtle"* (BE-G cat. no. 30) incorporates a relief form within a rectangular frame under a fence of wire; four eyes look out from the belly of the turtle. Mystical turtle objets d'art "swim" in a series of works from 1991, 1992, and 1998. The earlier works are encrusted with turtle shell, coral, glass, and beads; a family of turtle brooches from 1991— grandmother, father, mother, and child move ominously toward a being waiting to receive them (BE-G cat. no. 25). Turtles made of humble modeling clay are richly encrusted with gold leaf and paint: all at once, the dark gloomy reptiles become elegant ornaments worthy of another tradition.

In the midst of an intense exchange, we become aware that time has halted our visit. Our taxi arrives and Davira and I leave this secret world above a dusty road and travel back toward the reality of an urban Tel Aviv. We are en route to the Eretz Israel Museum and the presentation of "The Andy" award. The audience is an amazing mixture of Israelis and Americans from the cultural community.[13]

Epilogue

Henry James suggested that biographical data was among the great observed adventures of mankind; to "live history" is a privilege. For three days, Davira Taragin and I bore witness to the lives of four Israeli women artists. Two, Deganit Stern Schocken and Vered Kaminski, are first-generation Israelis whose parents emigrated from Europe to Israel. Two, Esther Knobel and Bianca Eshel-Gershuni, came as young children, from Poland and Bulgaria, respectively. All four are conjoined by their creative lives and their recognition of the independence that Israel has given to them as women and artists.

This journey is over; we have returned to Jerusalem. Davira is off to a meeting at the Israel Museum, and Deganit has sent me to meet with Danny Rubinstein, the foreign correspondent of *Haaretz*. History is in the making next to us as we dine in the American Colony Hotel and observe James D. Wolfensohn, the Middle East Envoy for The White House, negotiating a hopeful peaceful solution for the Palestinian-Arab dilemma with his staff. Before we go to the airport, Danny Rubinstein provides me with a quick automobile tour of the walled city, where we quickly pass the entrance to the cemetery where Oskar Schindler is buried. I am at once back in the summer of 1983 (when my late husband, Maurice English, and I came upon his grave site for the first time—long before the film was made). I remember leaving a stone, in the tradition of the Jewish religion, to note our presence, and I quietly think that perhaps this time I should have left four stones—one in each of the studios— as pledges of a swift return.

13. The Andrea M. Bronfman Prize for the Arts established by Charles Bronfman in honor of his wife and in support of Israeli decorative arts, to be given annually.

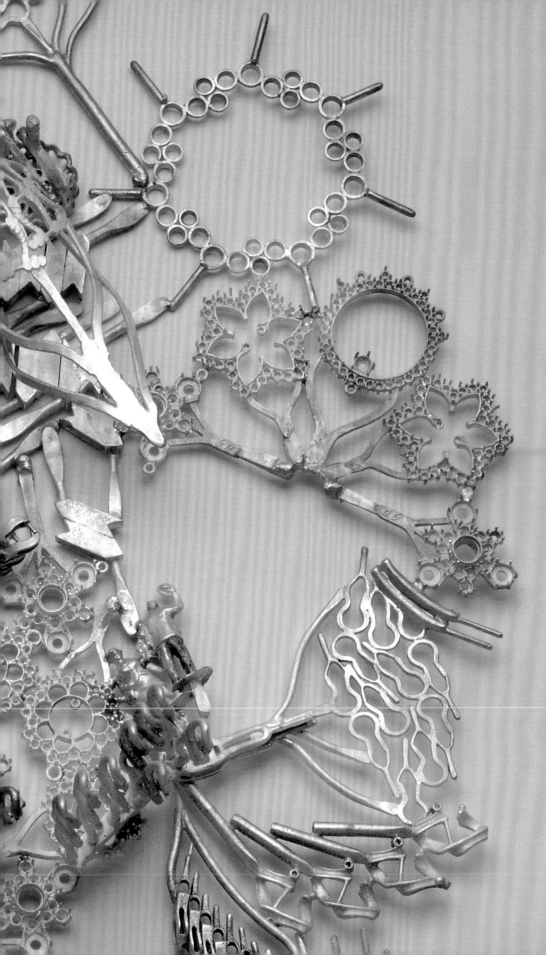

The Artists

Bianca Eshel-Gershuni

Vered Kaminski

Esther Knobel

Deganit Stern Schocken

Bianca Eshel-Gershuni

The debate regarding the hierarchical positioning of the fine and the applied arts has long been and remains a controversial one in Israel. When Bianca Eshel-Gershuni had a one-woman exhibition of her jewelry at The Israel Museum, Jerusalem, in 1977, curator Yona Fischer presented her work as artistic, but had a difficult time situating it within high and applied art. In Eshel-Gershuni's solo exhibition at The Tel Aviv Museum in 1985, curator Sara Breitberg-Semel described the artist as "alien to the dominant values of Israeli Art."[1]

Eshel-Gershuni was a pioneer. When she began to make jewelry for herself, with no formal training, she developed her own techniques for working in soft metals (BE-G cat. no. 18). Her early metal work (BE-G cat. no. 1) is reminiscent of the fused jewelry of the British jeweler Gerda Flöckinger, the early welded sculptures of Israeli Igael Tumarkin, and the jewelry and sculptures of the Italian Pomodoro brothers. The intimate touch of her hands on the soft materials, the gentle molding and rubbing, remains upon the final product. She works freely with both precious and common materials, including gold, plastic, feathers, pearls, aluminum foil, and Scotch-Brite (BE-G cat. no. 10).

Eshel-Gershuni mixes personal stories with pagan, folklore, and Christian motifs that express the personal, primeval voice of memories of love, loss, war, motherhood, and the reality of her life. For example, girlish dreams such as picking the petals of the daisy are expressed in *"He Loves Me, He Loves Me Not"* (BE-G cat. no. 11). Such a piece is an outgrowth of Israeli children's games such as pulling the seed of the stork's bill, which would curl up like a screw, and wearing it in a buttonhole as makeshift jewelry; another seed, the wrinkled medick, made small earrings. Some pieces approach kitsch or even fetishes (BE-G cat. no. 16). The erotic flirtation

between jewelry and the body is an important issue for Eshel-Gershuni. She works the back side of her jewelry, the part in contact with the body, claiming that any piece not worked on both sides is partially dead.

During the Gulf War, Eshel-Gershuni heard nightly the sound of sirens while she was engaged in producing a series of fish brooches. Reflecting on the finished pieces, she suddenly realized that she had unconsciously shaped one of her anthropomorphic works into a combat plane, manipulating sample bottles of men's cologne into missiles. From the belly of the reposing body of the plane in *Brooch* from 1991 (BE-G cat. no. 21) peeks a photograph of the artist. No doubt she was subconsciouly reminded of her pilot husband, who had tragically died in the Sinai Campaign of 1956.

Throughout her long career, Eshel-Gershuni has been an inspiration to many, particularly Vered Kaminski and Esther Knobel. Her highly personal work contains expressions of the pain and sorrow she has experienced. Motherhood and family, including her relationship with her own mother, have been focal points in her life and work. Early examples reflect her anger and frustration with her mother's passivity and silence. In her later works, however, she began not only to come to terms with her mother, but also to identify aspects of herself in her mother,[2] for example, *"Once There Was a Blue Turtle and My Mother Kept Silent Like a Turtle"* (BE-G cat. no. 30). Although she has embraced the personal, Eshel-Gershuni adamantly rejects being classified in a feminist niche, saying that she refuses to enter this ghetto of women art.[3] It is important to her that male motifs coexist with the feminine imagery in her work.

Although her art has no political message, Eshel-Gershuni made an exception in 1994, when she participated in the Sculpture Biennial at Tel Hai. For her *In*

Fig. 4 Bianca Eshel-Gershuni
You Are Beautiful—You Are the Most Beautiful—My Mother Said So, 1996
Modeling clay, aluminum foil, and paint
17 3/4 × 23 5/8 × 23 5/8 inches
Collection of the artist
©Photographer: Uri Gershuni, Tel Aviv

1. Hadara Scheflan-Katzav, "Relics of Something Sacred," *Studio Art Magazine* 66 (November-December 1995), p. 22.

2. Ibid., p. 25.

3. Sara Breitberg-Semel, "A Conversation with Bianca Eshel-Gershuni," *Studio Art Magazine* 66 (November-December 1995), p. 15.

Regards to the Roaring Lion, she substituted a roaring turtle for the lion, invoking the Trumpeldor Lion and thus, like others of her generation, ridiculing the sanctification of war and the history they had been taught as children.

In the early 1990s, Eshel-Gershuni began to imbue her images of turtles with her personal anxieties of aging and mortality. This decade-long series began with jewelry and gradually evolved into large sculptural pieces (fig. 4). She alternates between periods of working on jewelry and working on sculpture. There is always an overlap: moving fluidly between jewelry's intimate and detailed scale to larger sculptural pieces is a natural transition for her, and she views the two art forms as equals. In 2004, she became fascinated by the horse, after modeling one for her grandson. Never intending to create a realistic version, she first gave the forms wings. This led to her making a combination of Pegasus and a unicorn that she colored deep blue, red, and white, thereby giving it another layer of meaning. AW

Biography

1932 Born Sofia, Bulgaria

1939 Immigrated to Palestine

Education

1958–64 Avni Institute of Fine Arts, Tel Aviv

Selected One-Person Exhibitions

2005 Artists' House, Tel Aviv, "A Turtle's Journey" (exh. brochure)

1994 Memorial Center Gallery of Art, Qiryat Tivon, "Works 1985–1994" (exh. brochure)

1993 Sara Levi Gallery, Tel Aviv, "The State of the Turtle" (exh. brochure)

1985 The Tel Aviv Museum, "Bianca Eshel-Gershuni 1980–1985" (exh. cat.)

1977 The Israel Museum, Jerusalem, "Jewelry, Bianca Eshel-Gershuni" (exh. cat., traveled to Kunstindustrimuseet: The Danish Museum of Decorative Art, Copenhagen)

Selected Group Exhibitions

1994 Internationalen Handwerksmesse, Munich, "Schmuckszene '94"

1991 Museum of Israeli Art, Ramat Gan, Israel, "Place"

1991 Tel Aviv Museum of Art, "Israeli Art Now"

1991 The Genia Schreiber University Art Gallery, Tel Aviv University, "'The Absent Presence': The Empty Chair in Israeli Art" (exh. cat.)

1988 Brooklyn Museum, New York, "40 Israeli Artists" (exh. cat.)

1985 The Tel Aviv Museum, "Two Years 1983–84: Israeli Art–Qualities Accumulated" (exh. cat.)

1984 The Israel Museum, Jerusalem, "Eighty Years of Sculpture" (exh. cat.)

1982 The Israel Museum, Jerusalem, "Here and Now" (exh. cat.)

1982 Stadtische Kunsthalle, Düsseldorf, "Bilder sind nicht verboten" (exh. cat.)

1978 The Tel Aviv Museum, "Artist-Society-Artist" (exh. cat.)

1977 The Israel Museum, Jerusalem, "Jewelry 1900–1976 from the Collection of the Pforzheim Jewelry Museum" (exh. cat.)

1966 Gordon Gallery, Tel Aviv, "The Ten Plus Group"

Katz Gallery, Tel Aviv, "The Ten Plus Group"

Selected Collections

Gaby Brown, Tel Aviv

The Israel Museum, Jerusalem

The Israel Phoenix Assurance Company Ltd., Tel Aviv

Schmuckmuseum, Pforzheim, Germany

Hillela Tal, Israel

Tel Aviv Museum of Art

Selected Fellowships and Awards

1996–97 Israel Ministry of Education Prize

1993 The Israel Discount Bank Prize for Israeli Artists,
       The Israel Museum, Jerusalem

1960s–70s Jewelry Design Competitions, The Israeli
            Export Institute, first prize

1971 Internationalen Handwerksmesse, Munich,
      first prize

1 Bianca Eshel-Gershuni
   Necklace, 1971
   24k and 18k gold, pearls, and rubies
   Cat. no. 5

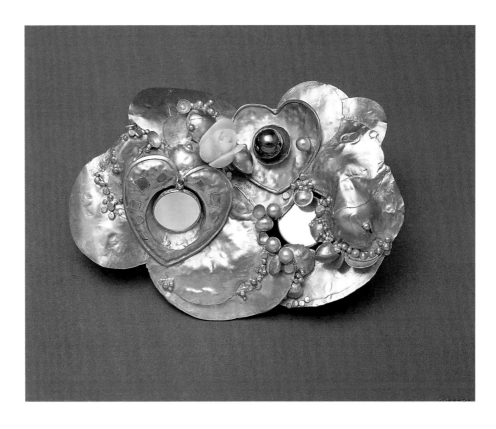

2   Bianca Eshel-Gershuni
Belt Buckle, 1973
18k gold, pearls, semiprecious
stones, porcelain, and mirrors
Cat. no. 7

3   Bianca Eshel-Gershuni
Pendant, 1974
18k gold, black pearl, coral, mirrors,
and white gold
Cat. no. 8

4   Bianca Eshel-Gershuni
Pendant, 1975
18k and 24k gold, pearls, camera
lens, onyx, and beads
Cat. no. 9

5   Bianca Eshel-Gershuni
    "He Loves Me, He Loves Me Not,"
    1976
    18k and 24k gold, jade, plaster,
    pearls, and plastic
    Cat. no. 11

6   Bianca Eshel-Gershuni
    "My Grave," Ring, 1977
    18k and 24k gold, plastic, plaster,
    feathers, pearls, and paint
    Cat. no. 13

7   Bianca Eshel-Gershuni
    Two Finger Ring, 1977
    18k and 24k gold, white coral,
    feathers, mirror, and plastic
    Cat. no. 14

8   Bianca Eshel-Gershuni
    "Go Bride Toward Your Groom,"
    1979–80
    Paint, shells, photograph, metal,
    plastic, fiber, and match box flowers
    Cat. no. 15

9 Bianca Eshel-Gershuni
   Pendant, 1980
   Paint, burlap, shells, plastic, and
   photograph
   Cat. no. 16

10 Bianca Eshel-Gershuni
   Earring, ca. 1980
   Shell, aluminum foil, feathers,
   metal, and glass beads
   Cat. no. 17

11 Bianca Eshel-Gershuni
    Brooch, 1985
    18k and 24k gold, jade, pearls,
    enamel, turquoise, coral, and onyx
    Cat. no. 18

12 Bianca Eshel-Gershuni
    Brooch, 1990
    24k gold leaf, copper, camel tooth,
    glass, and paint
    Cat. no. 20

13 Bianca Eshel-Gershuni
Brooch, 1991
Mirror, shell, silver, paint, photo-
graph, 24k gold, found objects, and
pearls
Cat. no. 21

14 Bianca Eshel-Gershuni
(clockwise from left)
Brooch, 1991
Mirror, shell, silver, paint, photo-
graph, 24k gold, found objects, and
pearls
Cat. no. 21
Brooch, 1991
Silver, fiber, glass, and paint
Cat. no. 23
Brooch, 1991
Silver and paint
Cat. no. 24
Brooch, 1991
Silver, paint, shell, turquoise, pearl,
and plastic
Cat. no. 22

15 Bianca Eshel-Gershuni

   *"Once There Was a Blue Turtle and
   My Mother Kept Silent Like a Turtle,"*
   1995
   Paint, aluminum foil, net, paper,
   and Masonite

   Cat. no. 30

53

16 Bianca Eshel-Gershuni
Turtle, Brooch, 1998
Modeling clay, 24k gold leaf, paint, and metal
Cat. no. 31

17 Bianca Eshel-Gershuni
Brooch, 2005
22k gold, silver, and lapis lazuli
Cat. no. 34

Vered Kaminski

Vered Kaminski has managed to maintain a balance between her personal work and her teaching as a senior lecturer at the Bezalel Academy of Art and Design, Jerusalem, since 1988. Skill in her art is part of Kaminski's psyche. Informed by the discipline of a long and formal education, she is steeped in the language of jewelry. The scale of jewelry is important to her, as it is also to Knobel and Stern Schocken. All three create micro worlds that engender intimate and physical encounters.

Kaminski clearly prefers hand-making, rather than manufacturing using industrial processes. In many ways, she is a silent virtuoso. Although her work demands a great deal of skill and patience, Kaminski views her method as meditative. Her design process involves well-defined and careful step-by-step research into materials and form. In her studio is an old cupboard—a treasure trove—that contains series upon series of exercises exploring different variations on a theme (fig. 5). She constantly reassembles fragments in order to form unique new pieces that share a common genetic identity (VK cat. nos. 21 a and d). In a brooch series from 1998, Kaminski manipulated mosaic patterns from silver and stainless steel, and, through a process of duplication and division mirroring cellular mitosis, created kaleido-scopic "snowflake" designs (VK cat. no. 22).

While studying in Paris in the years 1986–88, Kaminski became fascinated by her observation of what she perceived to be the French obsession with minutia, and began to concentrate more on details in her own work, causing her pieces to become more refined and delicate. Upon her return to Israel, she began to intro-duce into her jewelry local materials, such as gravel stones she found in the streets of Jerusalem (VK cat. no. 9). A series of brooches from the early 1990s, composed of cast concrete embedded with nickel silver, stainless steel, and brass (VK cat. no. 15), was clearly inspired by the way in which gravel and concrete are used in local building construction. The concrete functions simultaneously as a liquid stone and a setting material, giving Kaminski considerable flexibility in her work.

Kaminski is interested in the way one material can imitate another, but at the same time, she also plays with the value of materials. For example, in two silver cast brooches, in which she also utilized the front and back surfaces to produce two unique pieces, although the gravel has been replaced by expensive materials, the composition still recalls building sites (VK cat. no. 24).

Through noticing the texture of stones on the streets or in the façades of buildings, Kaminski moved toward an exploration of pattern. This preoccupation with duplication and repetition of motifs led, in turn, to an interest in the intricate arrangements and structures of Oriental design. Pieces from her bracelet series of 1998 (VK cat. nos. 19, 20) represent fences of enclo-sure with no beginning and no end, hinting subtly at Israel's security situation. Observing the geometry of natural shapes and the "branches" of trees inspired Kaminski to experiment with using lines to create three-dimensional volume, as in her 2^9 from 1999 (VK cat. no. 23). Following along the path of weaving in space led her to develop a series of basket forms (VK cat. no. 6). One of her first wire baskets held a stone in its base—a logical expression of its roots to jewelry. The main thrust of her work has always been jewelry, and the series of baskets was a natural progression in working in a larger scale. AW

Fig. 5 Cupboard in Vered Kaminski's studio in Jerusalem, 2005
©Photographer: Vered Kaminski, Jerusalem

54

Biography

1953 Born Kibbutz Revadim, Israel

Education

1986–88 University of Paris VIII, Vincennes–Saint-Denis, M.A.

1979–80 Rietveld Academy, Amsterdam, postgraduate studies

1975–79 Bezalel Academy of Art and Design, Jerusalem, B.A.

Selected One-Person Exhibitions

1999 Periscope Gallery, Tel Aviv

1996 Galerie Ra, Amsterdam

1991 The Israel Museum, Jerusalem, "Vered Kaminski: New Objects and Jewelry"

1991 Galerie V & V, Vienna

Selected Group Exhibitions

2001 Bayerischer Kunstgewerbe-Verein e.V., Munich, "Mikromegas" (exh. cat., traveled to Galerie für angewandte Kunst, Munich; Musée de l'Horlogerie et de l'Émaillerie, Geneva; American Craft Museum, New York; Hiko Mizuno College of Jewelry, Tokyo; The Powerhouse Museum, Sydney; The John Curtin Gallery, Perth; Musei civici agli eremitani di Padova, Padua)

1999 The Israel Museum, Jerusalem, "Seventy Designers: In Tribute to Izzika Gaon" (exh. brochure)

1998 Eretz Israel Museum, Tel Aviv, "Studs of Silver: Israeli Jewelry" (exh. cat.)

1998 Royal Museum of Scotland, Edinburgh, "Jewellery Moves" (exh. cat.)

1996 Internationalen Handwerksmesse, Munich, "Schmuckszene '96"

1992 Musée des Arts Décoratifs, Paris, "IIIème Triennale du Bijou" (exh. cat.)

1990 Musée du Luxembourg, Paris, "Triennale Européenne du Bijou" (exh. cat.)

1987 Hôtel de Sens, Paris, "Biennale du Bijoux Contemporain" (exh. cat.)

1986 Galerie Pegotty, Paris (two-person exhibition)

1984 The National Museum of Modern Art, Kyoto, and The National Museum of Modern Art, Tokyo, "Contemporary Jewellery: The Americas, Australia, Europe and Japan"

1982 Schmuckmuseum, Pforzheim, Germany, "Schmuck 82—Tendenzen" (exh. cat.)

1981 Stedelijk Museum, Amsterdam, "Retrospective Françoise van den Bosch"

Galerie Neon, Brussels (two-person exhibition)

1980 Künstlerhaus, Vienna, "Schmuck International 1900–1980"

Selected Collections

The Israel Museum, Jerusalem

Musée des Arts Décoratifs, Paris

Okresni Museum, Turnov, Czech Republic

Pinakothek der Moderne, Munich

Spertus Museum, Chicago

Stedelijk Museum Schiedam, The Netherlands

Selected Fellowships and Awards

2004 Prize in Art and Design, Ministry of Science, Culture, and Sport, Israel

1996 International Judaica Competition, Jerusalem, second prize (shared with Esther Knobel)

1987 Alix de Rothschild Foundation Prize

1985–88 Postgraduate Scholarship Grant, The Government of France

1979 Prize of Excellence, Bezalel Academy of Art and Design, Jerusalem

1977 Shapiro Prize for Judaica

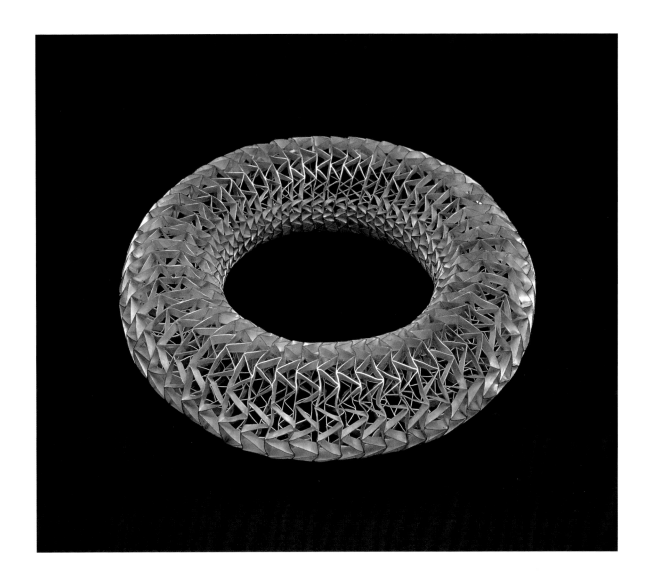

18 Vered Kaminski
Necklace, 1986
Silver
Cat. no. 2

19 Vered Kaminski
Bracelet, 1987
Silver
Cat. no. 3

20 Vered Kaminski
    Basket, 1991
    Stones and brass
    Cat. no. 6

21 Vered Kaminski
   Basket, 1991
   Stones and brass
   Cat. no. 8

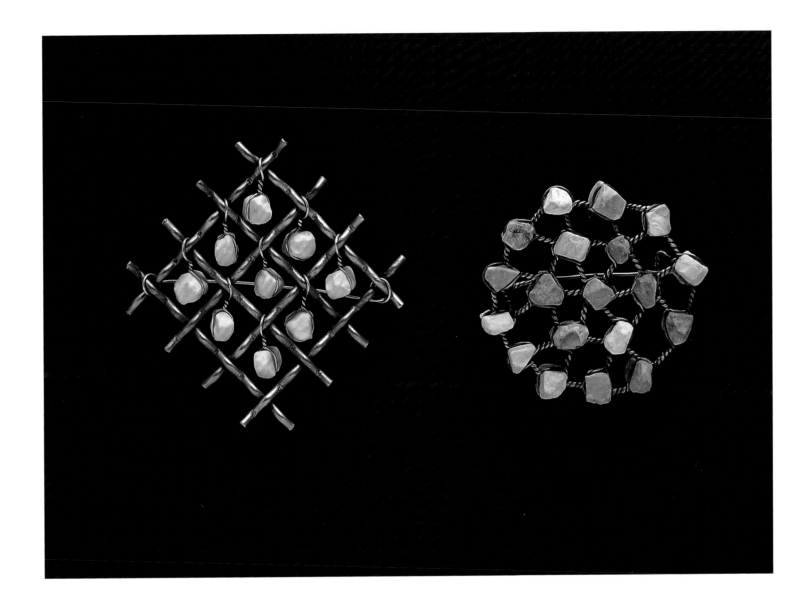

22 Vered Kaminski
    Brooch, 1991
    Galvanized steel, 18k gold,
    and stones
    Cat. no. 10
    Brooch, 1991
    Stones and nickel silver
    Cat. no. 9

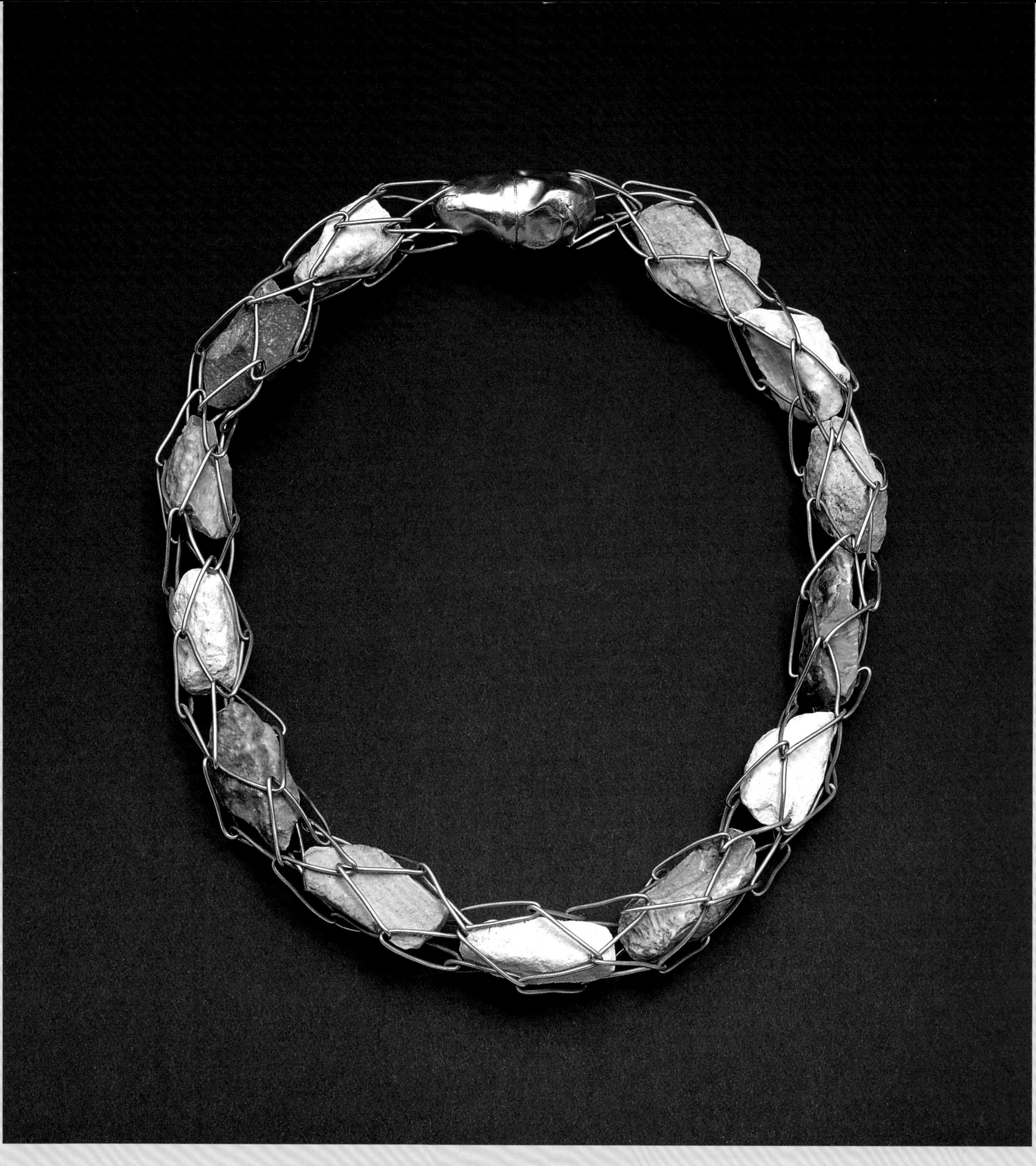

23 Vered Kaminski
    Necklace, 1991
    18k gold and stones
    Cat. no. 11

24 Vered Kaminski
    Brooch, 1992
    Stone, stainless steel, and silver
    Cat. no. 13

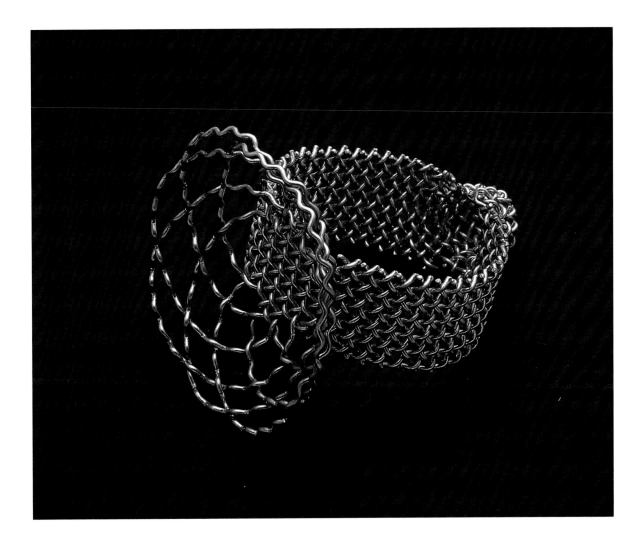

65

25 Vered Kaminski
    Brooches, 1992
    (a) Concrete, nickel silver, and
    stainless steel
    (b) Concrete, brass, and
    stainless steel
    Cat. no. 15

26 Vered Kaminski
    Bracelet, 1996
    Silver
    Cat. no. 16

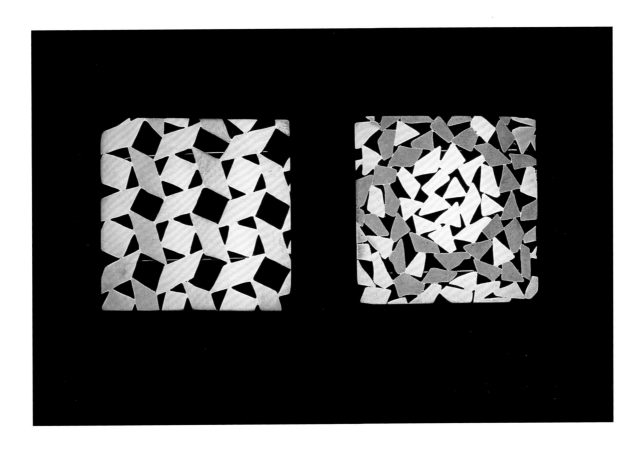

28 Vered Kaminski
Brooches, 1996
(a) Copper, brass, nickel silver, and stainless steel
(b) Copper, silver, and stainless steel
Cat. no. 18

27 Vered Kaminski
Bowl, 1996
Silver
Cat. no. 17

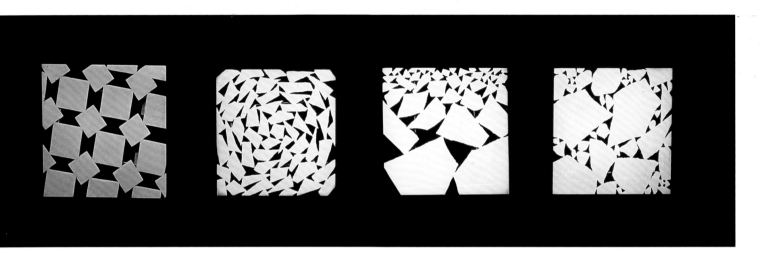

29 Vered Kaminski
    Brooches, 1998
    Silver and stainless steel
    (a)–(d)
    Cat. no. 21

30 Vered Kaminski
    2^9, 1999
    Brass
    Cat. no. 23

31 Vered Kaminski
    Brooches, 2000
    Silver and stainless steel
    (a) (b)
    Cat. no. 24

32 Vered Kaminski
    Necklace, 2001
    Anodized aluminum
    Cat. no. 25

33 Vered Kaminski
    (a) *Bracelet*, 2003
    Silver
    (b) *Bracelet*, 2004
    Silver
    (c) *Bracelet*, 2003
    Copper
    Cat. no. 26

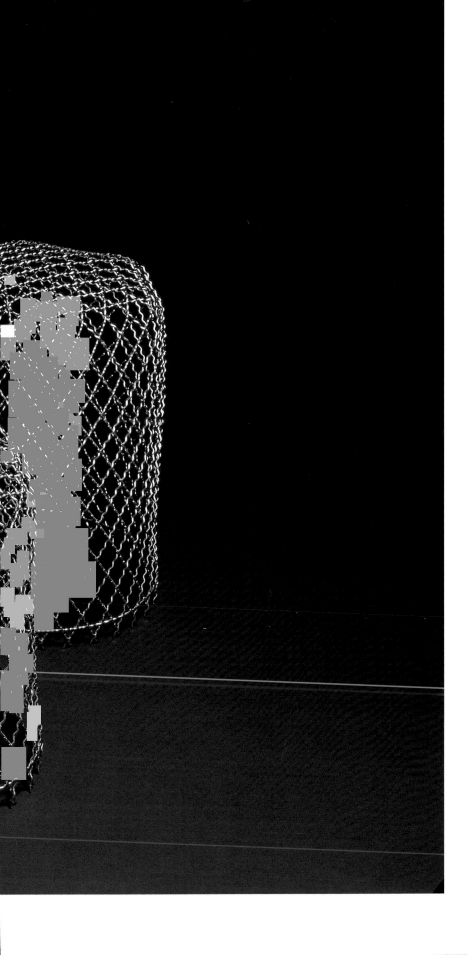

34 Vered Kaminski
    Stacking Stools, 2004
    Stainless steel
    (a)–(c)
    Cat. no. 27

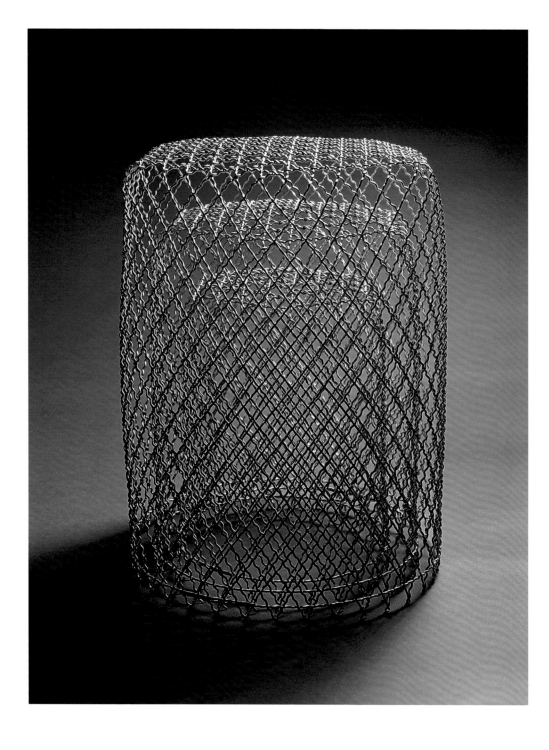

35 Vered Kaminski
    Stacking Stools, 2004
    Stainless steel
    Cat. no. 27

76

36 Vered Kaminski
2⁶ x 2 Earrings, 2005
Silver
Cat. no. 28

Esther Knobel

Throughout her studies at Jerusalem's Bezalel Academy and at the Royal College of Art in London, Esther Knobel searched for ways to connect personally to the area of jewelry. In her final year at Bezalel, she became aware of new developments in Dutch jewelry, especially the work of Gijs Bakker and Emmy van Leersum. Their reductive, simple geometric forms enabled the functional elements of the jewelry—how it locks, for example—to become part of the ornament. Following the path of architectural Modernism, some Dutch jewelers believed that contemporary jewelry should be more connected to the industrial world. Although Knobel produces one-offs, she always sees her work as capable of being produced in quantity, and in some cases she has used industrial processes. Beginning in the 1980s, Knobel participated in the European New Jewelry movement and her work was included in major exhibitions of the period.

Seeking to define her own direction and develop deeper personal content in her work, in London Knobel designed aluminum necklaces based on the shapes of pine needles, recalling the chains—the jewels—she made outdoors as a child. *Pine Tree Needles* (EK cat. no. 1), which is secured with a loop and tension mechanism, prompted Knobel to develop her own version of the safety pin (EK cat. no. 2). This series reveals her design approach: a search for purity of form through simple, imaginative solutions. The *Deck Chair* brooches (EK cat. no. 3) that followed were much more three-dimensional and demonstrate Knobel's practice of transforming a familiar object into a piece of jewelry. The nostalgic *"Tene"* baskets (EK cat. nos. 17, 18) recapture childhood festival memories of carrying fruit and vegetables to school in shoeboxes decorated with flowers.

Knobel's interest in color and pattern grew out of experimentation with anodized titanium, which led to the use of recycled tin, and eventually painting on tin.

The figurative *Archer* brooches marked a complete and significant departure from her previous work, opening up narrative in varied ways, initiating a dialogue with memory, and introducing iconic images as metaphors. She also began to explore the use of cold joints, embossing, and cut-outs. Moving from the single figure, Knobel then produced the *Sportsmen* necklaces in which the repetition of one element results in an overall abstract pattern (EK cat. no. 9). She became fascinated with warriors, explaining that she "was searching for strong archetypes, symbols recognizable by everyone." A work such as *Camouflage Necklace* (EK cat. no. 7), a wreath of camouflage-painted leaves, is ornamental but elegiac, evoking funeral wreaths and ceremonies for fallen soldiers—a strong comment on the reality of living in Israel.

In the 1990s series *Immigrants Brooches* (EK cat. nos. 23, 24), Knobel cut images of people, tigers, and rabbits from tin Chinese tea boxes, and balanced them upon tiny wheels or beams. Although seemingly playful, these compositions allude to the plight of the immigrant. Another inspiration—a photograph of her young son—resulted in *"The Prince" Handpiece* (EK cat. no. 16) and, so he would not be alone, the *"Mother" Handpiece* (EK cat. no. 14). These works gave rise to a series of portrait brooches set with small, semiprecious stones. Unlike goldsmiths and jewelers of the late sixteenth century, who painted portraits commissioned by important members of society, Knobel created her own clients.

Throughout her career, Knobel has maintained a prolific output of work that is constantly evolving and changing directions. She is active in exhibiting abroad, participating in international events, and giving workshops. In some instances, this exposure has introduced her to a new medium. For example, when she worked at *.ekwc*, the Europees Keramisch Werkcentrum in 's-Hertogenbosch, The Netherlands, in 1993, she

Fig. 6 Esther Knobel
Dedicated to Keren, 1999
Iron
Hamar, Norway
©Photographer: Gunnar Klingwall, Atelier Klingwall, Norway

experimented with porcelain and clay. At the Addenda 11 International Art Symposium in Hamar, Norway, in 1999, she explored cast iron as an artistic medium, making sculpture. This was also the first time Knobel worked on such a large scale. One of the sculptures was a vase, *Dedicated to Keren,* placed in a solitary location on the outskirts of the local cemetery (fig. 6). Knobel carved floral motifs into the sand mold, taken from an industrial readymade form, before it was cast in iron. The readymade has always played an important role in the work of Knobel, who has used it either as an integral part of her art or as a starting point of inspiration. AW

Biography

1949 Born Bielawa, Poland

1951 Immigrated to Israel

Education

1975–77 Royal College of Art, London, M.A.

1970–74 Bezalel Academy of Art and Design, Jerusalem, B.A. degree

1968–69 Institute for Plastic Arts, Bat Yam, Israel

Selected One-Person Exhibitions

1995 The Israel Museum, Jerusalem, "Refined Imagination: Esther Knobel, Jewelry" (exh. cat.)

1994 Galerie Ra, Amsterdam (exh. cat.)

1993 The Scottish Gallery, Edinburgh

1988 Galerie Spektrum, Munich

1984 Arnolfini, Bristol, United Kingdom

1983 Galerie Ra, Amsterdam

Selected Group Exhibitions

2003 Stedelijk Museum, Amsterdam, "BLUR"

2002–2003 Museum Het Kruithaus, 's-Hertogenbosch, The Netherlands, "Sense of Wonder" (exh. cat., traveled to Salone del Mobile, Milan, and Beurs van Berlage, Amsterdam)

2001 Bayerischer Kunstgewerbe-Verein e.V., Munich, "Mikromegas" (exh. cat., traveled to Galerie für angewandte Kunst, Munich; Musée de l'Horlogerie et de l'Émaillerie, Geneva; American Craft Museum, New York; Hiko Mizuno College of Jewelry, Tokyo; The Powerhouse Museum, Sydney; The John Curtin Gallery, Perth; Musei civici agli eremitani di Padova, Padua

1996 Royal College of Art, London, "Design of the Times: One Hundred Years of the Royal College of Art" (exh. cat., ed. Christopher Frayling and Claire Catterall)

1995 Province of Antwerp, "Sieraad, symbool, signaal = The Jewel: Sign and Symbol" (exh. cat.)

1991 Judisches Museum, Frankfurt am Main, "Jehi Or" (exh. cat.)

1989 Schmuckmuseum, Pforzheim, Germany, "Ornamenta I" (exh. cat.)

1987 Museum Francisco Carolinum, Linz, Austria, "Schmuck, Zeichen am Körper"

1984 Museum of Arts and Sciences, Sydney, "Cross Currents: Jewellery from Australia, Britain, Germany and Holland" (exh.cat., traveled throughout Australia and to New Zealand)

1983 Crafts Council Gallery, London, "The Jewellery Project: New Departures in British and European Work 1980–83" (exh. cat.)

1982 British Crafts Centre, London, "Jewellery Redefined: First International Exhibition of Multi-Media Non-Precious Jewellery" (exh. cat.)

1982 Crafts Council Gallery, London, "The Maker's Eye" (exh. cat.)

Selected Collections

Art Gallery of Western Australia, Perth

The Israel Museum, Jerusalem

Museum für angewandte Kunst (MAK), Vienna

Museum of Arts & Design, New York

The Museum of Fine Arts, Houston, Helen Williams Drutt Collection

National Museum of Scotland, Edinburgh

Racine Art Museum, Wisconsin

Stedelijk Museum, Amsterdam

Selected Fellowships and Awards

1999   Israel Ministry of Science, Culture, and Sport Prize in Art and Design

1996   International Judaica Competition, Jerusalem, second prize (shared with Vered Kaminski)

1994   Françoise van den Bosch Prize, The Netherlands

1993   America-Israel Cultural Foundation Grant, residency at the Europees Keramisch Werkcentrum, 's-Hertogenbosch, The Netherlands

1975   British Council Scholarship for the Royal College of Art

37 Esther Knobel
Pine Tree Needles, 1977
Anodized aluminum
Cat. no. 1

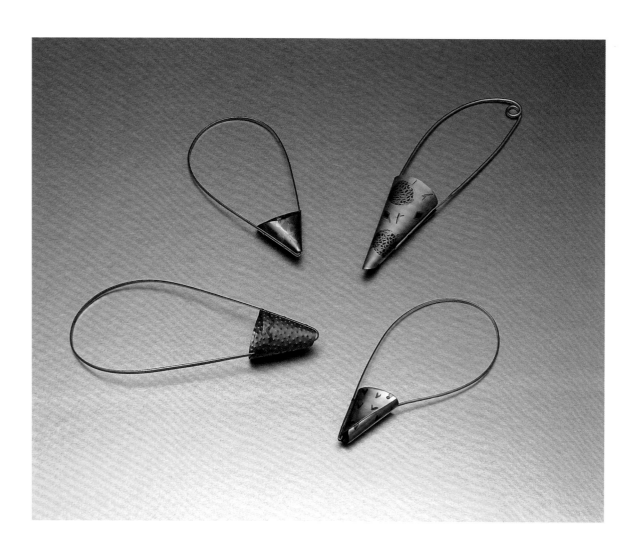

38 Esther Knobel
Safety Pins, 1977
Anodized titanium and stainless steel
(clockwise from left)
(a)–(d)
Cat. no. 2

39 Esther Knobel
Snail Brooches, 1981
(clockwise from left)
Cat. no. 4b
Recycled tin can
(a)–(c)
Cat. no. 4a
Anodized titanium
(a)

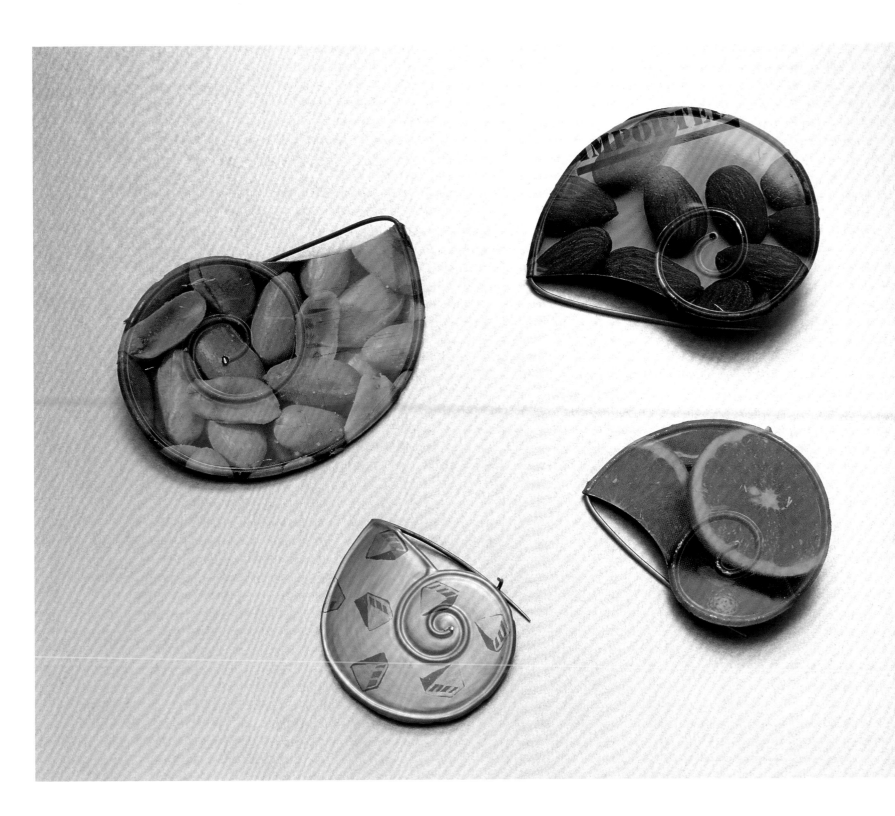

84

85

40 Esther Knobel
Camouflage Necklace, 1982
Recycled tin can, fabric, paint,
ribbon, textile, and silk cord
Cat. no. 7

41 Esther Knobel
Warrior on Horse Brooch, 1983
Recycled tin can, paint, and
stainless steel
Cat. no. 8

42 Esther Knobel
Sportsmen Neckpiece, 1985
Recycled tin can and paint
Cat. no. 9

87

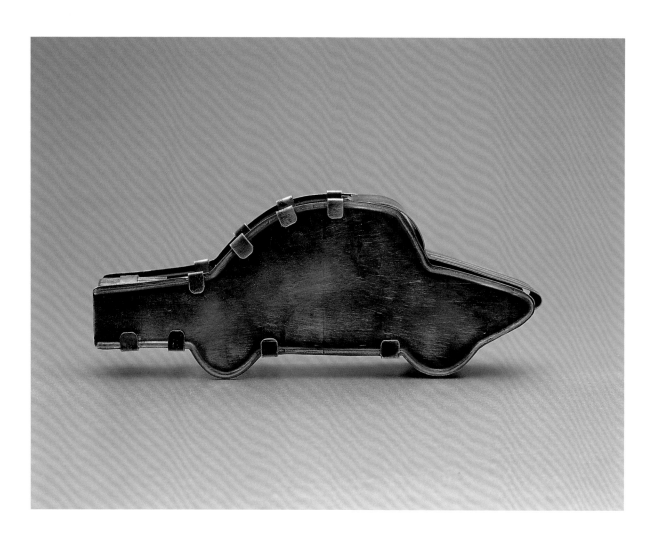

43 Esther Knobel
    Car Brooch, 1987
    Nickel silver, fabric, paint, and
    plastic
    Cat. no. 11

44 Esther Knobel
    Pendant, 1987
    Nickel silver, fabric, and paint
    Cat. no. 12

45 Esther Knobel
   "The Prince" Handpiece, 1989
   Nickel silver
   Cat. no. 16

46 Esther Knobel
   "Tene" Basket, 1991
   Nickel silver
   Cat. no. 17

47 Esther Knobel
    "Rabbit in Pram" Brooch, 1992
    Nickel silver
    Cat. no. 21

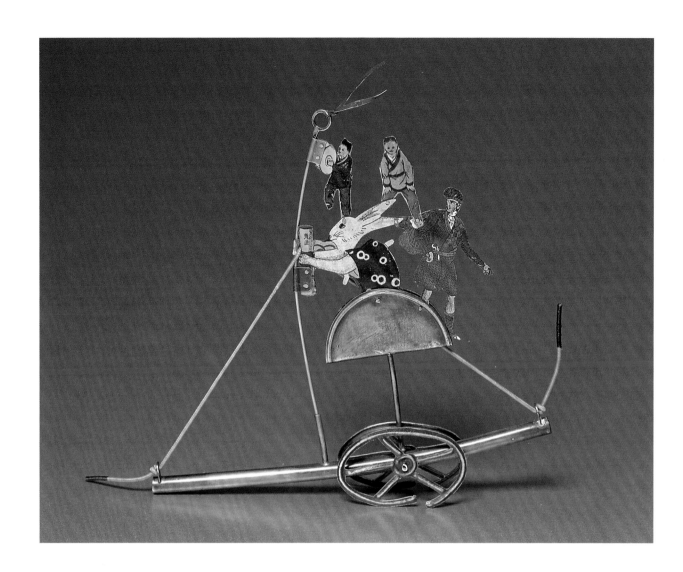

48 Esther Knobel
Daisy Wire, 1993
Silver and 18k gold
Cat. no. 22

49 Esther Knobel
Immigrants Brooch, 1993
Recycled tin can, nickel silver, elastic
band, and stainless steel
Cat. no. 23

50 Esther Knobel
    Requiem, 1994
    Copper, brass, and thread
    (a)–(p)
    Cat. no. 25

51 Esther Knobel
    "Bride" Necklace, 1994
    Silver and laminated paper and
    petals
    Cat. no. 26

52 Esther Knobel

"My Grandmother Is Knitting Too,"
2000

Enameled copper

Top row (a)–(c);
bottom row (d)–(h)

Cat. no. 30

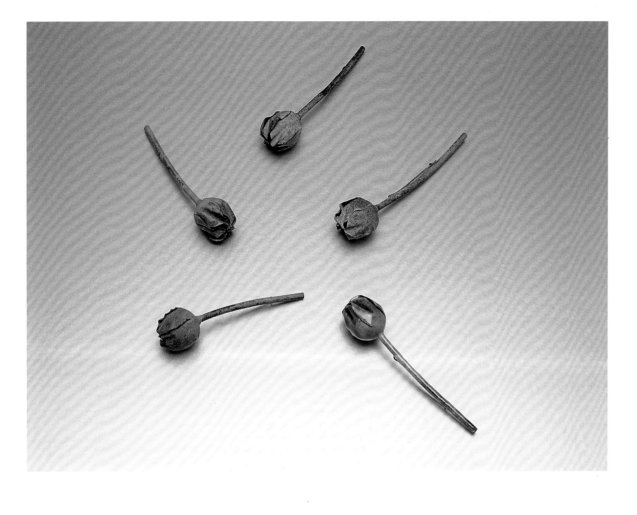

53 Esther Knobel
   Tulip Brooches, 2000
   Enameled copper
   (clockwise from lower left)
   (a)–(e)
   Cat. no. 31

54 Esther Knobel
   A Kit for Mending Thoughts, 2005
   18k and 24k gold, silver, paper,
   and tin
   Cat. no. 33

Deganit Stern Schocken

The earliest examples of Deganit Stern Schocken's jewelry are finely crafted largely in traditional materials. Interested in extending her vocabulary, she soon began to experiment with nontraditional materials, including stones, paper, plastics, and readymade objects, such as cookie molds. At the same time, she began to question the role of jewelry on the body.

Fragmentation is a constant element in her work. The interaction between jewelry and the wearer inspired the *Brooch* series of the 1980s (DSS cat. nos. 1, 5), in which movement and change are emphasized. The pin and hinged elements become the focus of attention, whereas normally they are hidden and of secondary importance. Here, however, they are manipulated to engage the wearer in a play with movement (DSS cat. no. 2). In Stern Schocken's *Body Pieces* (DSS cat. nos. 13–16), each item resembles an independent built structure, but arranged together the elements commune with each other like the parts of a whole organism, laid out like the plan of a city. What interests Stern Schocken in these works is the fact that when worn, portions of her pieces are hidden from the sight of both the viewer and the wearer. In all her work, the pieces are meant to be seen off as well as on the body.

In several series of brooches, Stern Schocken explores the notion of the gemstone. In traditional jewelry, the setting of the stone is influenced by the preciousness of the stone itself. In a series from the early 1990s, Stern Schocken substituted fabric for the stone (DSS cat. nos. 11, 12). Similarly, in the later, shimmering, water-inspired *Pools* series (DSS cat. no. 17), the focus is on the negative space of the "empty" settings and the full visual impact of the stone is revealed only when water fills the "setting."

Already in her early jewelry, Stern Schocken addressed line, plane, and mass using language directly linked to architecture. The intersection of two- and three-dimensional elements recalls aerial views of urban landscapes. She continued to explore landscape, along with rich surface textures, in a series of landscape brooches from 1996 that reflect the spirit of her drawings (DSS cat. nos. 23–25). Nonetheless, the artist is primarily occupied with objects in space rather than linear configuration and with specific examples from her local environment: the buildings of Tel Aviv's "White City"—a collection of neighborhoods featuring buildings designed in the distinctive clean geometry of the Bauhaus style (fig. 7). Stern Schocken's study of architecture at the Bezalel Academy of Art and Design also must have influenced her direction.

The artist has described her jewelry as miniature architecture on the body, and in 1995, she expanded her scale, and began working on installations. This departure from jewelry into other artistic media is not unusual, since some jewelers, such as Claus Bury from Germany and Susanna Heron from England have felt that the scale of jewelry is often too restrictive. Recently, Stern Schocken presented her installation *How Many Is One* at the Tel Aviv Museum. Such crossing over between the disciplines of craft and fine arts has, however, caused a great deal of debate over the years. One question that occurs with regard to Stern Schocken's work is whether the presentation is more important than the content of the work itself.

Since 2000 Stern Schocken has chaired the department of jewelry at the Shenkar College of Engineering and Design, Ramat Gan. AW

Fig. 7 Ze'ev (Wilhelm) Haller (Israeli, born Germany, 1882–1956)
Bruno House, 1935
3 Strauss Street, Tel Aviv
©Photographer: Yigal Gawze, Tel Aviv

100

Biography

1947 Born Kibbutz Amir, Israel

Education

2001–2002 Middlesex University, London, M.A.

1977–78 Middlesex Polytechnic (Hornsey School of Art), London

1974–76 Sir John Cass School of Art, London

1972–73 Bezalel Academy of Art and Design, Jewelry Department, Jerusalem

1968–72 Bezalel Academy of Art and Design, Department of Industrial Design and Architecture, B.A.

Selected One-Person Exhibitions

2003 Tel Aviv Museum of Art, "How Many Is One: Deganit Stern Schocken" (exh. cat.)

1998 Galería Alfredo Melgar, Madrid

1996 Galerie Ra, Amsterdam, "Replacements"

1993 Galerie Equinoxe, Geneva

1991 Bertha Urdang Gallery, New York

1984 Helen Drutt Gallery, Philadelphia

Selected Group Exhibitions

2002 Eretz Israel Museum, Ramat Aviv, "Chain Reaction: Israeli Jewelry II" (exh. cat.)

2001 The Israel Museum, Jerusalem, "Love at First Sight: The Vera, Silvia, and Arturo Schwarz Collection of Israeli Art" (exh. cat. by Arturo Schwarz)

2000 Galerie Ra, Amsterdam, "MaskeRade: Contemporary Masks by Fifty Artists" (exh. cat.)

1998–2001 Helen Drutt, Philadelphia, "Broaching It Diplomatically: A Tribute to Madeleine K. Albright" (exh. cat. by Wendy Steiner; traveled to Museum Het Kruithuis, 's-Hertogenbosch, The Netherlands; Museum of Art and Design, Helsinki; Tarbekunstimuuseum, Tallinn, Estonia; Museum of Contemporary Art, Oostende, Belgium; American Craft Museum, New York; The Contemporary Museum, Honolulu; Philadelphia International Airport; Villa Croce, Genoa, Italy, Kunstgewerbemuseum, Berlin; Schmuckmuseum, Pforzheim, Germany

1997 Ein Hod Sculpture Biennale, Ein Hod, Israel, "Humanisim 2020? The Fourth Biennale" (exh. cat.)

1996 New Central Bus Station Mall, Tel Aviv, "'Bubbles': Station Transformation—Project No. 3"

1995 Office in Tel Aviv, "Deganit Stern Schocken" (two-person exhibition; exh. cat. by Rachel Sukman)

1994 Office in Tel Aviv, "Tel Aviv in the Tracks of the Bauhaus" (exh. cat.)

Tower of David Museum of the History of Jerusalem, Jerusalem, "Local Goddesses" (exh. cat.)

1992 Musée des Arts Décoratifs, Paris, "IIIème Triennale du Bijou" (exh. cat.)

1990 Internationalen Handwerksmesse, Munich, "Schmuckszene '90"

Musée du Luxembourg, Paris, "Triennale Européenne du Bijou" (exh. cat.)

1987 Deutsches Goldschmiedehaus Hanau, Hanau, Germany, "Schmuck in Bewegung, Bewegung in Schmuck"

Selected Collections

Brooklyn Museum, New York

The Israel Museum, Jerusalem

The Museum of Fine Arts, Houston, Helen Williams Drutt Collection

Nordenfjeldske Kunstindustrimuseum, Trondheim, Norway

Racine Art Museum, Wisconsin

Selected Fellowships and Awards

2001 Alix de Rothschild Foundation Prize

1997 Israel Ministry of Education and Culture Prize for the Encouragement of Artists in the Field of Plastic Arts and Design

1990 Commendation, "Signatures: International Jewellery Competition 'Aus Gold und Silber,'" Stadtischen Museum, Schwäbisch Gmünd, Germany

1977 Commendation, De Beers Competition, *Diamonds Tomorrow 1977*, London

55 Deganit Stern Schocken
Brooch, 1981
Silver
Cat. no. 2

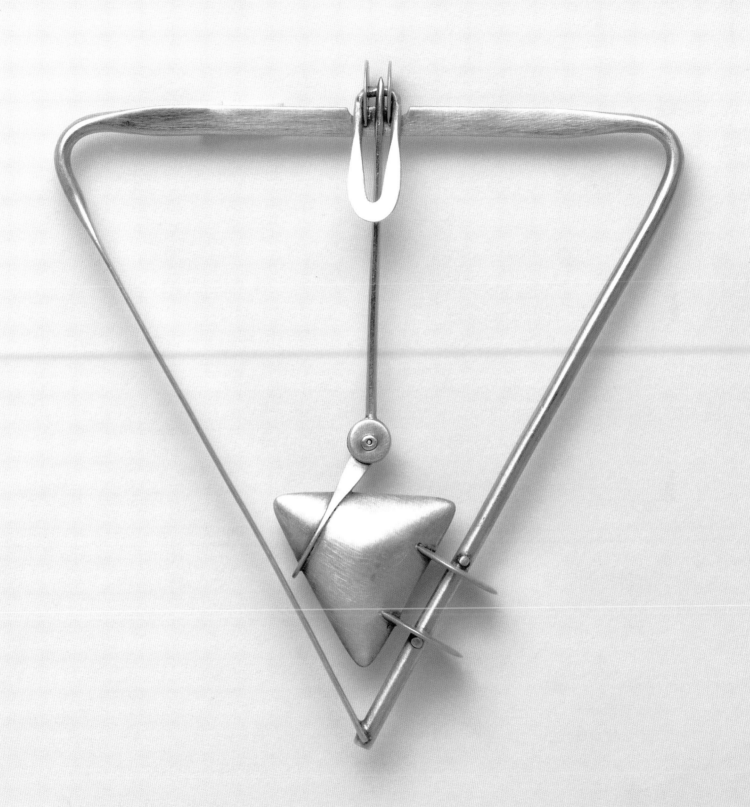

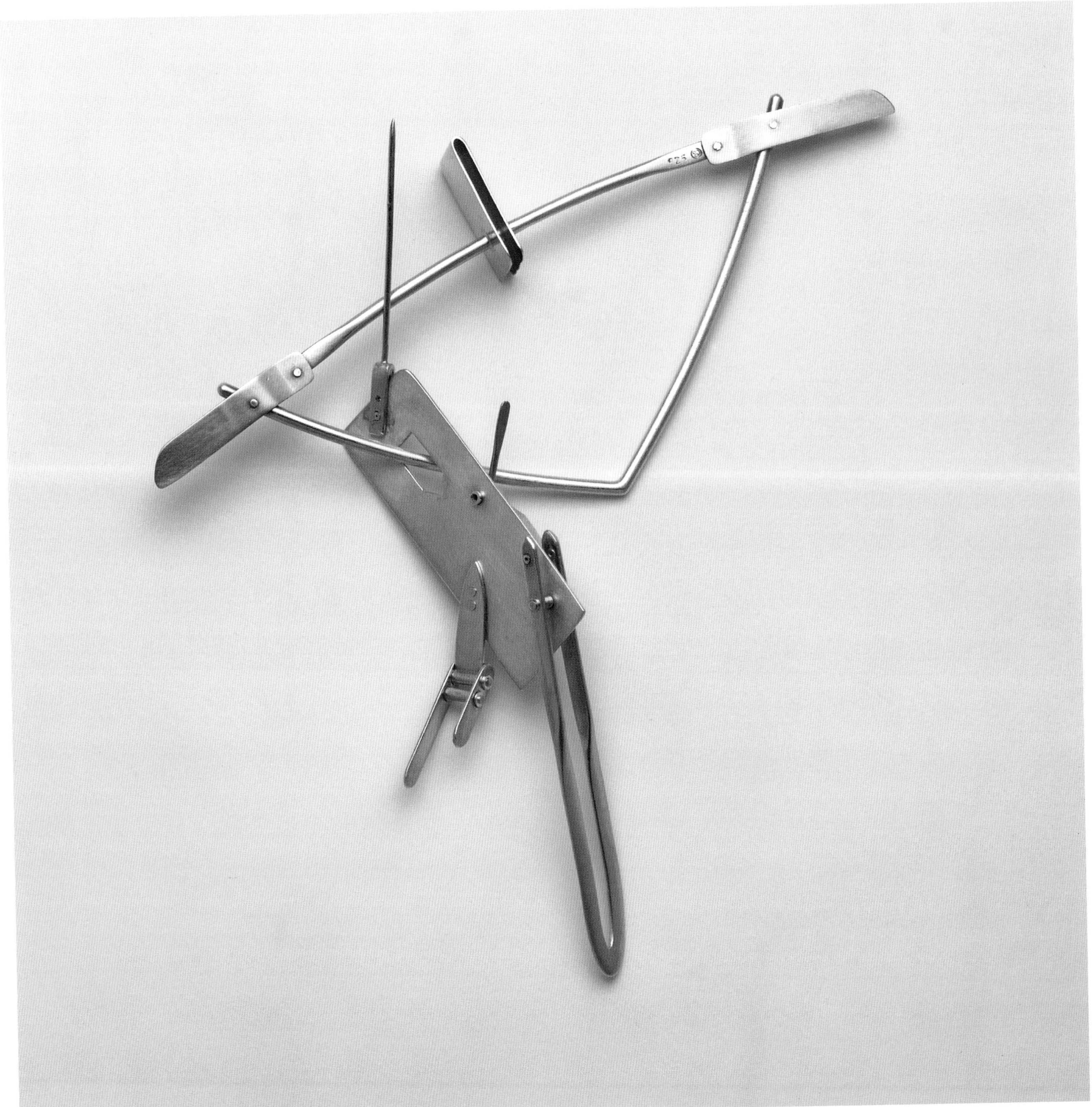

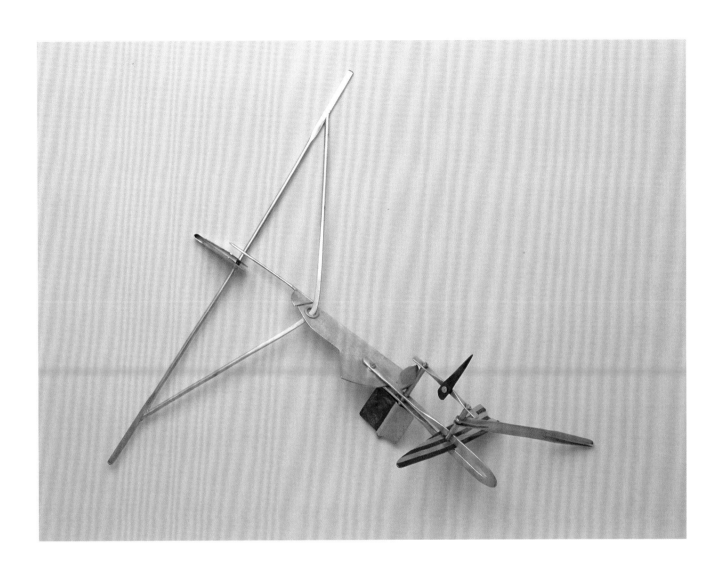

56 Deganit Stern Schocken
   Brooch, 1987
   Silver and 18k gold
   Cat. no. 4

57 Deganit Stern Schocken
   Brooch, 1987
   Copper and silver
   Cat. no. 5

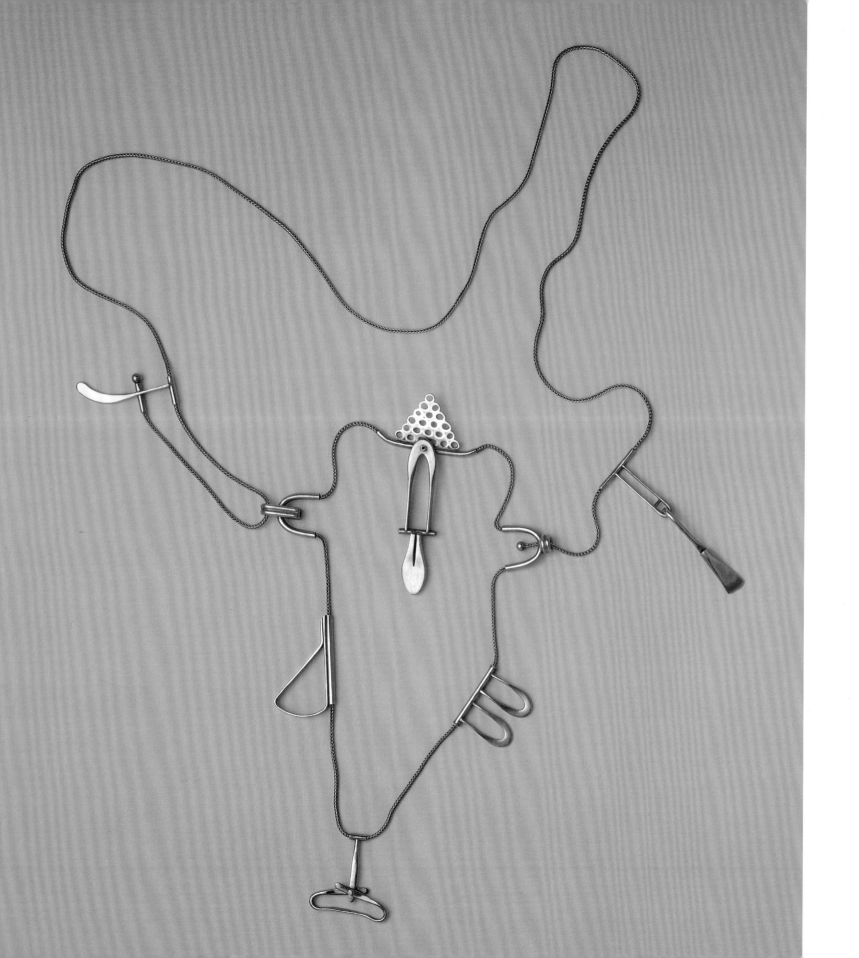

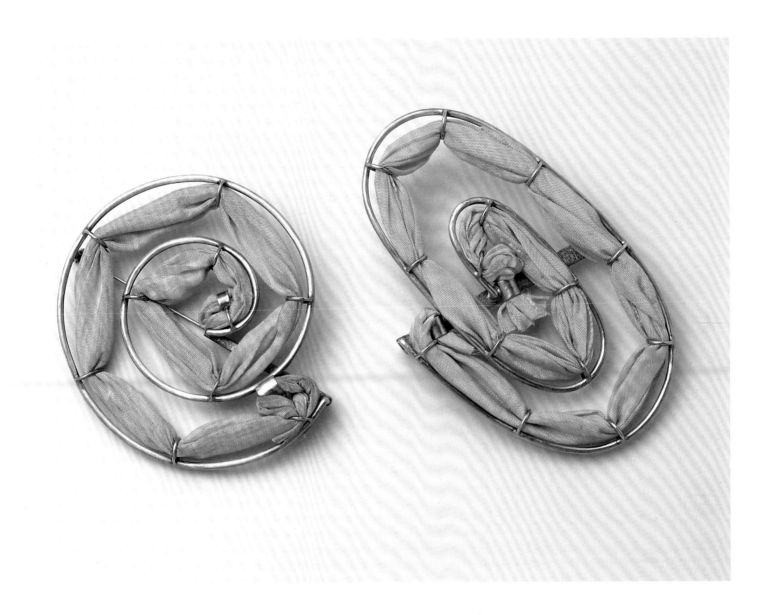

59 Deganit Stern Schocken
Brooch, 1990
Silver and silk
Cat. no. 11
Brooch, 1990
Silver and silk
Cat. no. 12

58 Deganit Stern Schocken
Neckpiece, 1988
Silver and 18k gold
Cat. no. 7

60 Deganit Stern Schocken
   Body Piece, 1992
   Silver, silk, semiprecious stones,
   stainless steel, and shell
   Cat. no. 13

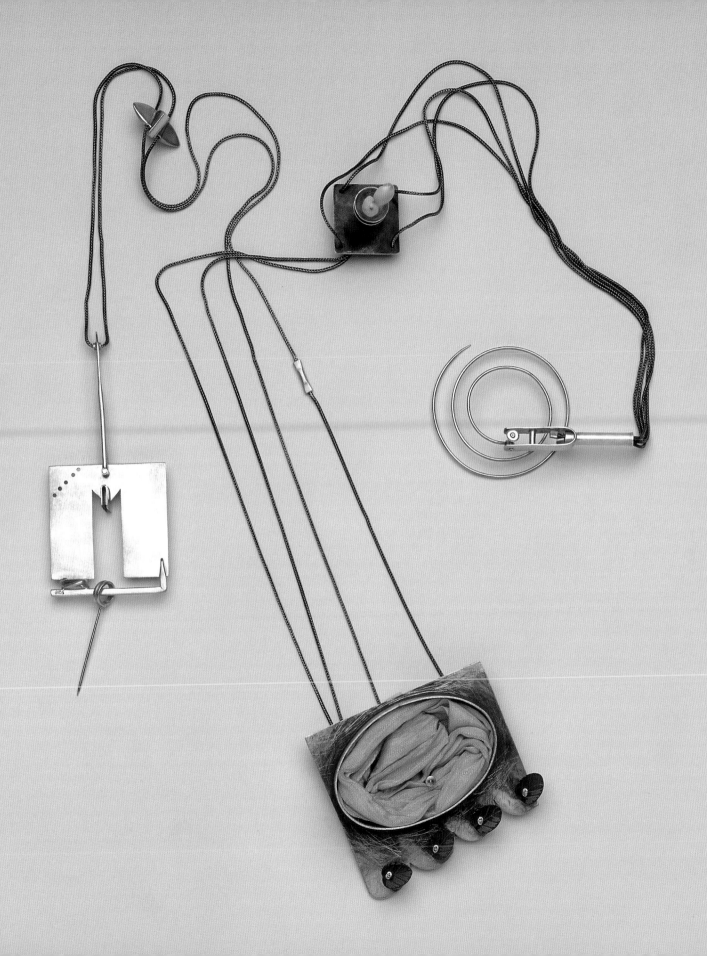

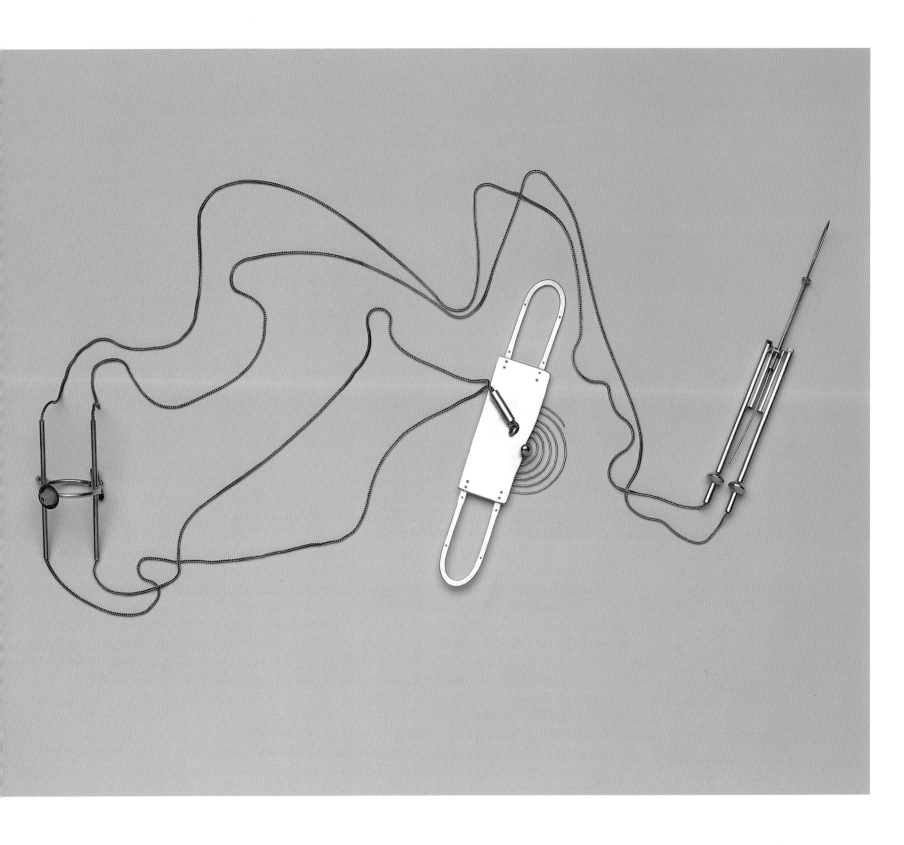

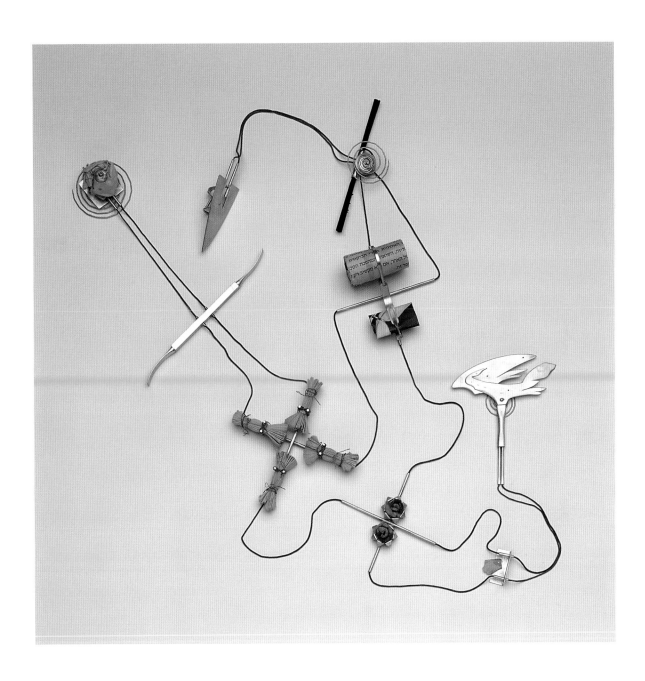

61 Deganit Stern Schocken
    Body Piece, 1993
    Nickel silver, semiprecious stones,
    stainless steel, copper, and
    18k gold
    Cat. no. 14

62 Deganit Stern Schocken
    Body Piece (City), 1993
    Nickel silver, stainless steel,
    paper, silver, and shell
    Cat. no. 16

63 Deganit Stern Schocken
Two Pools (Not Brooches), 1993
(a) Oxidized silver
(b) Silver
Cat. no. 17

64 Deganit Stern Schocken
Three Eye Brooches, 1995
(a) Silver and plastic
(b) Silver and jade
(c) Silver and jade
Cat. no. 19

how many is four, no 10

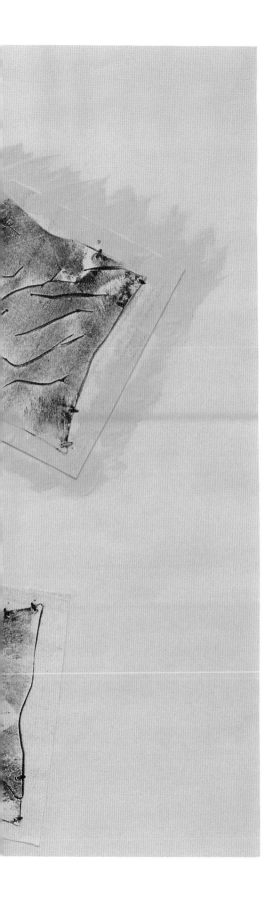

65 Deganit Stern Schocken
    How Many Is Four, No. 10, 1996
    Paper, cotton thread, and silver
    Cat. no. 22

66 Deganit Stern Schocken
Landscape Brooch, 1996
Silver, cotton thread, and quartz
(a) (b)
Cat. no. 24

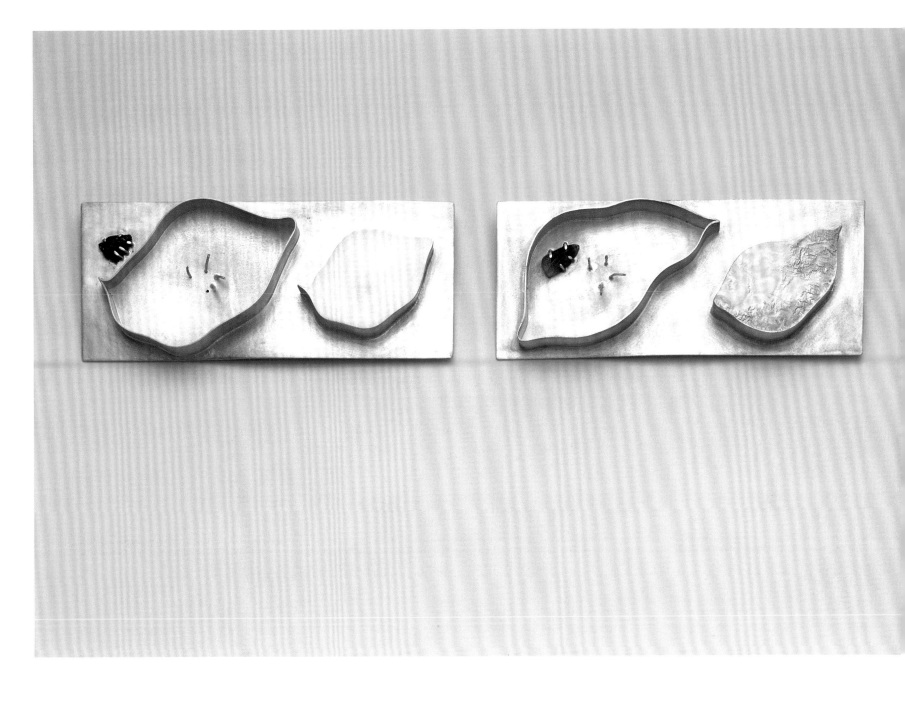

67 Deganit Stern Schocken
Landscape Brooch, 1996
Silver, 18k gold, and tourmaline
(a) (b)
Cat. no. 25

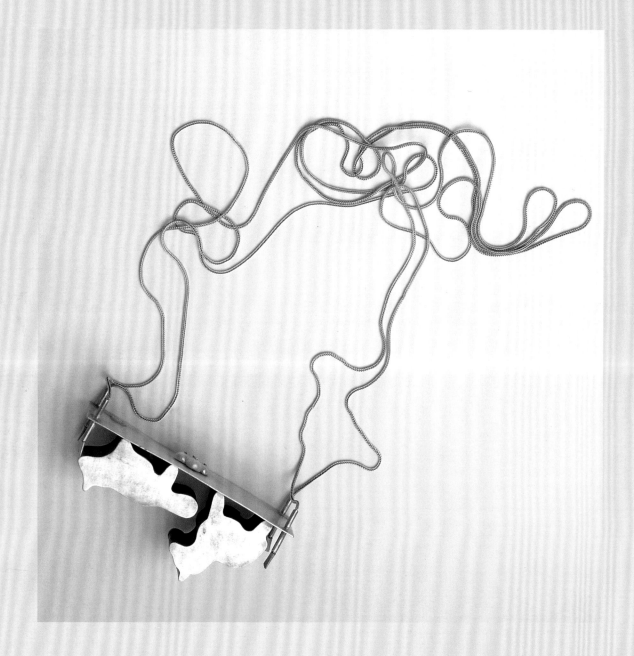

68 Deganit Stern Schocken
    Neckpiece, 1996
    Silver, pearls, and found object
    Cat. no. 26

69 Deganit Stern Schocken
    Neckpiece, 1996
    Silver, jade, amethyst, and
    semiprecious stones
    Cat. no. 27

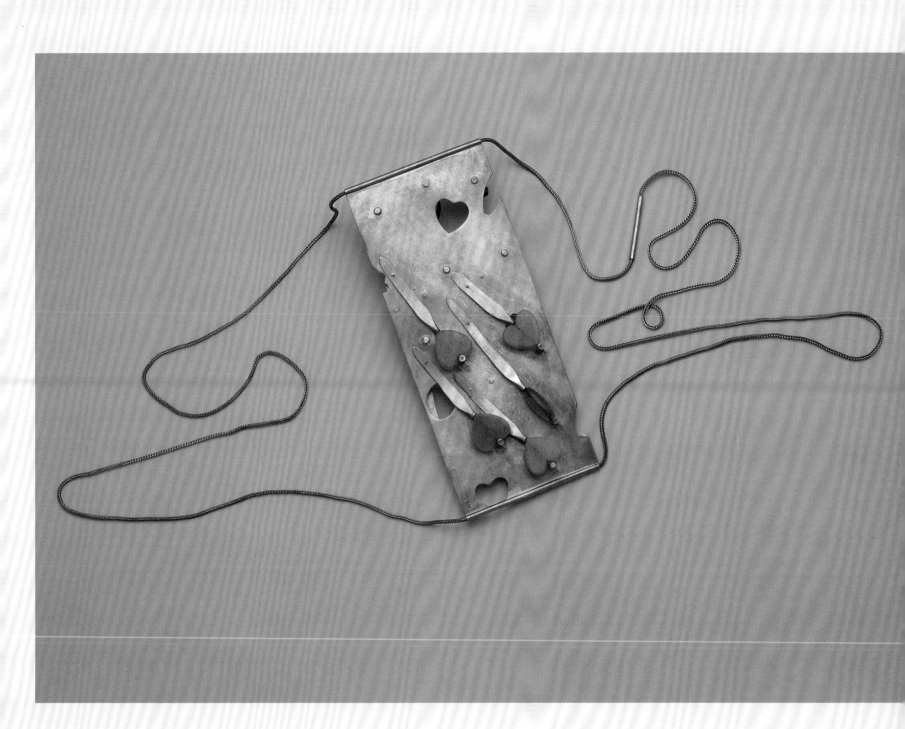

70 Deganit Stern Schocken
    City, 2003, from *How Many Is One*,
    2003–2004
    Silver and semiprecious stones
    Cat. no. 29

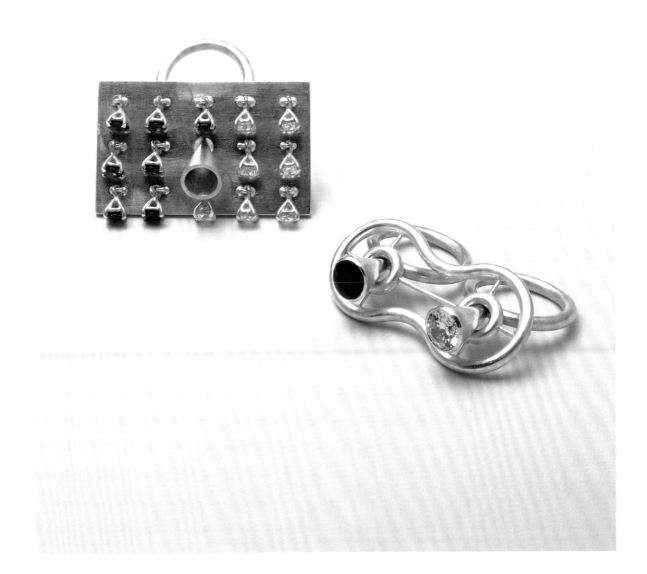

71 Deganit Stern Schocken
    How Many Is One, 2003–2004
    Silver, paint, and wax
    Forty-two pieces
    Cat. no. 30

72 Deganit Stern Schocken
    2 Rings, 2005
    Silver and semiprecious stones
    (a) (b)
    Cat. no. 32

Catalogue of the Exhibition

All objects are courtesy of the respective artists unless otherwise indicated. Dimensions are given in the following order: height or length followed by width and depth.

**Bianca Eshel-Gershuni
(born Sofia, Bulgaria, 1932)**

1. *Necklace with Pendant*, 1966
   Silver and semiprecious stones
   9 × 5 1/4 × 1 1/8 inches

2. *Necklace with Pendant*, 1966
   Silver
   Pendant: 3 1/4 × 5 × 1 inches
   Necklace with pendant:
   23 1/4 × 5 1/8 × 1 inches

3. *Pendant*, 1966
   Silver, glass, and cotton thread
   2 3/4 × 7 3/4 × 7/8 inches

4. *Bracelet*, ca. 1970
   18k gold, black pearl, and pearls
   3 × 2 3/4 × 1 5/8 inches

5. *Necklace*, 1971
   24k and 18k gold, pearls, and rubies
   8 × 6 × 1 1/2 inches
   Plate 1

6. *Ring for Three Fingers*, 1971
   18k gold, pearls, and rubies
   1 1/4 × 2 1/2 × 1 inches

7. *Belt Buckle*, 1973
   18k gold, pearls, semiprecious stones, porcelain, and mirrors
   10 1/2 × 4 1/4 × 1 inches
   Plate 2

8. *Pendant*, 1974
   18k gold, black pearl, coral, mirrors, and white gold
   4 1/2 × 6 × 1 5/8 inches
   Plate 3

9. *Pendant*, 1975
   18k and 24k gold, pearls, camera lens, onyx, and beads
   4 × 5 1/4 × 1 1/8 inches
   Plate 4

10. *Earring*, 1976
    18k and 24k gold, pearl, red coral, feathers, aluminum foil, and plastic
    9 1/2 × 8 5/8 × 1 inches

11. *"He Loves Me, He Loves Me Not,"* 1976
    18k and 24k gold, jade, plaster, pearls, and plastic
    (a)–(e) 2 × 2 1/4 × 1/2 inches
    (f) 8 1/2 × 2 3/4 × 2 inches
    Plate 5

12. *Ring*, 1976
    18k and 24k gold, asphalt, plastic, porcelain, and feathers
    3 3/4 × 6 1/4 × 2 inches

13. *"My Grave," Ring*, 1977
    18k and 24k gold, plastic, plaster, feathers, pearls, and paint
    2 1/2 × 4 3/4 × 1 1/2 inches
    Plate 6

14. *Two Finger Ring*, 1977
    18k and 24k gold, white coral, feathers, mirror, and plastic
    2 5/8 × 3 × 1 3/8 inches
    Plate 7

15. *"Go Bride Toward Your Groom,"* 1979–80
    Paint, shells, photograph, metal, plastic, fiber, and match box flowers
    5 1/2 × 7 × 1 1/2 inches
    Plate 8

16. *Pendant*, 1980
    Paint, burlap, shells, plastic, and photograph
    11 3/8 × 6 1/8 × 1 inches
    Plate 9

17. *Earring*, ca. 1980
    Shell, aluminum foil, feathers, metal, and glass beads
    12 1/4 × 10 1/2 × 1 1/4 inches
    Plate 10

18. *Brooch*, 1985
    18k and 24k gold, jade, pearls, enamel, turquoise, coral, and onyx
    4 1/2 × 4 1/2 × 1 1/4 inches
    Plate 11

19. *Brooch*, 1985
    24k gold, plastic, fur, metal, crystal, and paint
    4 3/4 × 3 5/8 × 1 1/4 inches

20. *Brooch*, 1990
    24k gold leaf, copper, camel tooth, glass, and paint
    3 1/2 × 3 3/4 × 1 inches
    Plate 12

21. *Brooch*, 1991
    Mirror, shell, silver, paint, photograph, 24k gold, found objects, and pearls
    6 × 4 7/8 × 1 1/2 inches
    Plates 13, 14

22. *Brooch*, 1991

Silver, paint, shell, turquoise, pearl, and plastic

6 1/2 × 4 1/8 × 1 inches

Plate 14

23. *Brooch*, 1991

Silver, fiber, glass, and paint

3 5/8 × 2 1/2 × 5/8 inches

Plate 14

24. *Brooch*, 1991

Silver and paint

2 × 3 3/8 × 3/4 inches

Plate 14

25. *Turtles*, 1991

(a) Turtle shell, metal, beads, silver, mirrors, found objects, and paint
2 7/8 × 4 1/2 × 3 1/2 inches

(b) Turtle shell, pearls, shell, silver, and modeling clay
1 5/8 × 4 1/8 × 2 7/8 inches

(c) Modeling clay, 24k gold, silver, tortoise shell, opals, beads, and pearls
1 1/4 × 3 1/8 × 2 1/8 inches

(d) Modeling clay, silver, 24k gold, glass beads, and shell
3/4 × 1 3/4 × 1 inches

26. *Turtle, Brooch*, 1992

Turtle shell, silver, 18k and 24k gold, coral, glass, beads, paint, and found objects

4 3/4 × 4 3/8 × 1 inches

27. *Brooch*, 1992–93

Silver, pearl, 24k and 18k gold, and shell

4 × 3 7/8 × 3/4 inches

28. *Caesar*, 1993

18k and 24k gold leaf, paint, glass, and bronze

3 3/4 × 3 5/8 × 3 3/4 inches

29. *Brooch*, 1994

Silver, 18k gold, and glass

3 5/8 × 3 5/8 × 3/4 inches

30. *"Once There Was a Blue Turtle and My Mother Kept Silent Like a Turtle,"*

1995

Paint, aluminum foil, net, paper, and Masonite

13 × 11 3/4 × 3 3/4 inches

Plate 15

31. *Turtle, Brooch*, 1998

Modeling clay, 24k gold leaf, paint, and metal

5 3/8 × 4 1/4 × 1 1/4 inches

Plate 16

32. *Turtle, Brooch*, 1998

Modeling clay, 24k gold leaf, and paint

4 1/4 × 4 × 1 inches

33. *Turtle, Brooch*, 1998

Modeling clay, paint, 24k gold leaf, pearls, and glass

4 3/4 × 3 7/8 × 3/4 inches

34. *Brooch*, 2005

22k gold, silver, and lapis lazuli

3 1/2 × 3 1/2 × 3/8 inches

Plate 17

**Vered Kaminski
(born Kibbutz Revadim, Israel, 1953)**

1. *Pendant*, 1987
Silver
2 1/8 × 2 1/8 × 2 1/8 inches

2. *Necklace*, 1986
Silver
15 7/8 × 1 5/8 × 1 3/4 inches
Collection of The Israel Museum, Jerusalem; Purchase, Palevsky Fund, B87.981
Plate 18

3. *Bracelet*, 1987
Silver
5 1/2 × 5 1/2 × 1 1/2 inches
Plate 19

4. *Necklace*, 1988
Silver
23 × 1 × 1 inches

5. *Brooch*, 1990
Stone, copper, and nickel silver
3 1/4 × 3 1/8 × 1/2 inches

6. *Basket*, 1991
Stones and brass
4 3/4 × 12 × 12 inches
Plate 20

7. *Basket*, 1991
Floor tiles and copper
5 5/8 × 19 × 19 inches
Collection of Michael Brennand-Wood, England

8. *Basket*, 1991
Stones and brass
8 × 15 × 15 inches
Collection of the Shenfeld Family, Israel
Plate 21

9. *Brooch*, 1991
Stones and nickel silver
2 1/2 × 2 1/2 × 1 5/8 inches
Plate 22

10. *Brooch*, 1991
Galvanized steel, 18k gold, and stones
3 1/4 × 3 1/4 × 1/2 inches
Plate 22

11. *Necklace*, 1991
18k gold and stones
19 1/8 × 3/4 × 3/4 inches
Plate 23

12. *Brooch*, 1991/92
Concrete, stainless steel, glass, and plastic
3/4 × 3 1/2 × 3/8 inches

13. *Brooch*, 1992
Stone, stainless steel, and silver
2 × 2 × 1/2 inches
Plate 24

14. *Brooch*, 1992
Nickel silver, copper, brass, and stainless steel
1/2 × 1 3/4 × 1/8 inches
Collection of Tom Kaminski, Jerusalem

15. *Brooches*, 1992
(a) Concrete, nickel silver, and stainless steel
1 3/8 × 1 3/8 × 3/8 inches
(b) Concrete, brass, and stainless steel
1 1/2 × 1 1/2 × 3/8 inches
Plate 25

16. *Bracelet*, 1996
Silver
4 3/8 × 3 × 3 inches
Plate 26

17. *Bowl*, 1996
Silver
3 7/8 × 7 3/4 × 7 3/4 inches
Plate 27

18. *Brooches*, 1996
(a) Copper, brass, nickel silver, and stainless steel
1 5/8 × 1 5/8 × 1/4 inches
(b) Copper, silver, and stainless steel
1 1/2 × 1 1/2 × 1/4 inches
Plate 28

19. *Bracelet*, 1998
Stainless steel
5 1/2 × 2 7/8 × 2 7/8 inches

20. *Bracelet*, 1998
Stainless steel
4 × 2 3/4 × 2 7/8 inches

125

21. *Brooches*, 1998
Silver and stainless steel
(a) 1 5/8 × 1 5/8 × 1/4 inches
(b) 1 5/8 × 1 5/8 × 1/4 inches
(c) 1 1/2 × 1 1/2 × 1/4 inches
(d) 1 1/2 × 1 5/8 × 1/4 inches
Plate 29

22. *Brooches*, 1998
Silver and stainless steel
(a) 1 1/4 × 1 5/8 × 1/4 inches
(b) 1 1/4 × 1 1/2 × 1/4 inches
(c) 1 1/2 × 1 5/8 × 1/4 inches
(d) 1 3/8 × 1 1/2 × 1/4 inches
(e) 1 3/8 × 1 3/8 × 1/4 inches
(f) 1 1/2 × 1 5/8 × 1/4 inches
(g) 1 1/2 × 1 1/2 × 1/4 inches

23. *2⁹*, 1999
Brass
10 1/2 × 18 × 16 inches
Collection of The Israel Museum,
Jerusalem. Gift of Vered Kaminski,
Jerusalem, B00.0060
Plate 30

24. *Brooches*, 2000
Silver and stainless steel
(a) 1 3/4 × 1 3/4 × 3/8 inches
(b) 1 5/8 × 1 5/8 × 3/8 inches
Plate 31

25. *Necklace*, 2001
Anodized aluminum
37 1/8 × 3/4 × 5/8 inches
Plate 32

26. *Bracelets*
(a) Bracelet, 2003
Silver
2 5/8 × 2 5/8 × 2 1/2 inches
(b) Bracelet, 2004
Silver
2 5/8 × 2 5/8 × 2 1/2 inches
(c) Bracelet, 2003
Copper
2 5/8 × 2 5/8 × 2 3/8 inches
Plate 33

27. *Stacking Stools*, 2004
Stainless steel
(a) 19 × 15 × 15 inches
(b) 13 × 10 × 10 inches
(c) 16 × 12 × 12 inches
Plates 34, 35

28. *2⁶ x 2 Earrings*, 2005
Silver
Each 2 1/2 × 3/4 × 3/4 inches
Collection of Donna Schneier
Plate 36

Esther Knobel
(born Bielawa, Poland, 1949)

1. *Pine Tree Needles*, 1977
Anodized aluminum
(a) 32 × 3/4 × 1/2 inches
(b) 34 × 3/4 × 1/2 inches
Plate 37

2. *Safety Pins*, 1977
Anodized titanium and stainless
steel
(a) 4 × 1 5/8 × 1/2 inches
(b) 3 × 1 5/8 × 1/4 inches
(c) 4 3/8 × 1 1/8 × 3/8 inches
(d) 3 1/4 × 1 5/8 × 3/8 inches
Plate 38

3. *Deck Chairs*, 1977–78
Anodized titanium and stainless
steel
(a) 2 × 3/4 × 5/8 inches
(b) 2 1/8 × 1 1/2 × 3/8 inches
(c) 2 7/8 × 3/4 × 5/8 inches
(d) 2 5/8 × 7/8 × 1 1/8 inches

4a. *Snail Brooches*, 1981
Anodized titanium
(a) 1 3/8 × 1 5/8 × 1/8 inches
(b) 2 5/8 × 1 7/8 × 1 1/16 inches
Plate 39

4b. *Snail Brooches*, 1981
Recycled tin can
(a) 1 7/8 × 2 5/8 × 1/8 inches

(b) 1 3/4 × 2 1/4 × 1/8 inches
(c) 1 1/2 × 1 7/8 × 1/8 inches
Collection of The Israel Museum,
Jerusalem; Purchase, Palevsky Fund,
B88. 423a, b, d
Plate 39

5. *Archer*, 1985
Recycled tin can and paint
6 1/2 × 3 1/2 × 1/4 inches
Collection of the Museum of Arts &
Design, New York. Gift of Donna
Schneier, 1997
On exhibition in the United States
only

Archer, 1984–85
Recycled tin can and paint
6 × 3 1/2 × 1/4 inches
Collection of The Israel Museum,
Jerusalem; Purchase, Palevsky Fund,
B88.422
On exhibition in Europe and The
Israel Museum, Jerusalem, only

6. *Crusader*, 1985
Recycled tin can and paint
5 × 6 1/2 × 1/4 inches
Collection of the Museum of Arts &
Design, New York. Gift of Donna
Schneier, 1997
On exhibition in the United States
only

Warrior on Horse, 1985
Recycled tin can and paint
7 1/8 × 4 3/8 × 1/4 inches
On exhibition in Europe and The
Israel Museum, Jerusalem, only

7. *Camouflage Necklace*, 1982
Recycled tin can, fabric, paint,
ribbon, textile, and silk cord
18 × 4 1/2 × 3/4 inches
Collection of the Museum of Arts &
Design, New York. Gift of Donna
Schneier, 1997
On exhibition at the Racine Art
Museum only
Plate 40

8. *Warrior on Horse Brooch*, 1983
Recycled tin can, paint, and stainless
steel
4 1/2 × 4 5/8 × 1/8 inches
Plate 41

9. *Sportsmen Neckpiece*, 1985
Recycled tin can and paint
20 1/2 × 3 3/4 × 1/4 inches
Plate 42

10. *Snake*, 1987
Nickel silver, paint, and fabric
28 3/8 × 1 1/8 × 3/4 inches

11. *Car Brooch*, 1987
Nickel silver, fabric, paint, and
plastic
1 7/8 × 4 5/8 × 7/8 inches
Plate 43

12. *Pendant*, 1987
Nickel silver, fabric, and paint
22 × 4 1/4 × 1 inches
Plate 44

13. *"Cotton" Scarf*, 1989
Nickel silver, waterproof fabric, and
cotton
38 3/8 × 3 1/8 × 1 3/8 inches

14. *"Mother" Handpiece*, 1989
Nickel silver
3 3/4 × 1 7/8 × 3/4 inches

15. *Pomegranate*, 1989
Nickel silver and nylon fabric
Belt: 37 3/4 × 4 × 1 1/2 inches
Scarf: 72 × 2 3/4 × 2 1/2 inches
Bracelets: 8 1/8 × 1 3/8 × 1 inches each

16. *"The Prince" Handpiece*, 1989
Nickel silver
4 5/8 × 2 × 1 inches
Plate 45

17. *"Tene" Basket*, 1991
   Nickel silver
   12 × 12 × 13 inches
   Plate 46

18. *"Tene" Basket*, 1992
   Brass, laminated cactus flowers, and eucalyptus leaves
   16 $^1/_2$ × 14 $^1/_2$ × 5 $^3/_4$ inches

19. *Hot Pepper Basket*, 1992
   Nickel silver and hot peppers
   9 $^1/_2$ × 12 $^1/_8$ × 12 $^1/_8$ inches

20. *"Precious Man" Brooch*, 1992
   Nickel silver, paint, gold and silver foil, 18k gold, and coral
   1 $^7/_8$ × 1 $^3/_4$ × $^5/_8$ inches

21. *"Rabbit in Pram" Brooch*, 1992
   Nickel silver
   3 $^1/_4$ × 3 $^1/_2$ × $^3/_4$ inches
   Plate 47

22. *Daisy Wire*, 1993
   Silver and 18k gold
   7 $^1/_2$ × 7 $^1/_2$ × 1 $^1/_4$ inches
   Plate 48

23. *Immigrants Brooch*, 1993
   Nickel silver, recycled tin can, elastic band, and stainless steel
   4 $^3/_4$ × 5 × $^1/_2$ inches
   Plate 49

24. *Immigrants Brooch*, 1993
   Nickel silver, recycled tin can, elastic band, and stainless steel
   4 $^5/_8$ × 6 × $^7/_8$ inches

25. *Requiem*, 1994
   Copper, brass, and thread
   (a) 1 $^3/_4$ × 1 $^1/_8$ × $^5/_8$ inches
   (b) 2 $^1/_4$ × 1 $^3/_8$ × $^5/_8$ inches
   (c) 2 $^1/_4$ × 1 $^1/_2$ × $^5/_8$ inches
   (d) 1 $^7/_8$ × 1 $^1/_2$ × $^5/_8$ inches
   (e) 2 $^3/_8$ × 1 $^1/_2$ × $^1/_2$ inches
   (f) 2 $^1/_8$ × 1 $^1/_2$ × $^1/_2$ inches
   (g) 2 $^1/_4$ × 1 $^3/_8$ × $^5/_8$ inches

(h) 2 × 1 $^1/_4$ × $^1/_2$ inches
(i) 2 $^1/_4$ × 1 $^3/_8$ × $^5/_8$ inches
(j) 2 $^1/_4$ × 1 $^1/_4$ × $^3/_4$ inches
(k) 1 $^5/_8$ × 1 $^1/_4$ × $^1/_2$ inches
(l) 2 × 1 $^1/_2$ × $^5/_8$ inches
(m) 2 × 1 $^1/_4$ × $^1/_2$ inches
(n) 2 × 1 $^1/_2$ × $^5/_8$ inches
(o) 1 $^7/_8$ × 1 $^1/_4$ × $^1/_2$ inches
(p) 1 $^1/_2$ × 1 $^1/_4$ × $^3/_4$ inches
Plate 50

26. *"Bride" Necklace*, 1994
   Silver and laminated paper and petals
   Pendant with chain: 23 $^3/_4$ × 5 × 1 $^1/_4$ inches
   Pendant: 4 × 2 $^3/_4$ × 1 $^1/_4$ inches
   Plate 51

27. *Jasmine Carpet*, 1995
   Copper
   27 $^3/_4$ × 27 $^3/_4$ × $^1/_8$ inches

28. *Dahlia Ring*, 1996
   Silver
   1 $^3/_4$ × 1 $^1/_8$ × 1 $^1/_8$ inches

29. *Seder Plate*, 1996
   Silver, wood, silk, and glass
   3 $^1/_8$ × 16 $^1/_2$ × 16 $^1/_2$ inches

30. *"My Grandmother Is Knitting Too,"* 2000
   Enameled copper
   (a) 4 $^1/_2$ × 2 $^1/_4$ × $^5/_8$ inches
   (b) 6 $^1/_2$ × 3 $^1/_2$ × 1 inches
   (c) 2 $^1/_2$ × 2 $^1/_2$ × $^7/_8$ inches
   (d) 1 $^3/_8$ × 1 $^3/_4$ × 1 inches
   (e) 1 × 1 $^5/_8$ × $^3/_4$ inches
   (f) 1 × $^3/_4$ × $^3/_4$ inches
   (g) 1 $^1/_2$ × 1 × 1 inches
   (h) 1 × 1 $^5/_8$ × 1 inches
   Plate 52

31. *Tulip Brooches*, 2000
   Enameled copper
   (a) 3 $^1/_2$ × $^7/_8$ × $^7/_8$ inches
   (b) 3 $^3/_4$ × $^7/_8$ × $^7/_8$ inches

(c) 3 $^7/_8$ × $^7/_8$ × $^7/_8$ inches
(d) 4 $^1/_4$ × $^7/_8$ × $^7/_8$ inches
(e) 4 × $^3/_4$ × $^3/_4$ inches
Plate 53

32. *Clematis*, 2002
   Nickel silver and laminated petals
   (a) 39 $^3/_4$ × 4 $^1/_8$ × $^1/_8$ inches
   (b) 42 × 5 × $^1/_8$ inches
   (c) 42 $^7/_8$ × 4 $^7/_8$ × $^1/_8$ inches
   (d) 37 $^1/_4$ × 3 $^7/_8$ × $^1/_8$ inches
   (e) 37 $^3/_4$ × 3 $^3/_4$ × $^1/_8$ inches
   (f) 38 × 4 $^1/_4$ × $^1/_8$ inches

33. *A Kit for Mending Thoughts*, 2005
   18k and 24k gold, silver, paper, and tin
   1 $^3/_{16}$ × 7 × 3 $^1/_8$ inches
   Plate 54

Deganit Stern Schocken
(born Kibbutz Amir, Israel, 1947)

1. *Brooch*, 1981
   Silver, gold wire, and rubber
   2 $^5/_8$ × 1 $^5/_8$ × $^1/_4$ inches

2. *Brooch*, 1981
   Silver
   2 $^3/_4$ × 2 $^1/_4$ × $^1/_4$ inches
   Plate 55

3. *Brooch*, 1986
   Silver and 18k gold
   1 $^3/_4$ × 2 $^3/_4$ × $^3/_8$ inches

4. *Brooch*, 1987
   Silver and 18k gold
   5 $^1/_4$ × 4 $^5/_8$ × 1 $^3/_8$ inches
   Plate 56

5. *Brooch*, 1987
   Copper and silver
   6 $^3/_4$ × 6 $^1/_2$ × $^7/_8$ inches
   Plate 57

6. *Brooch*, 1987
   Silver, copper, and plastic thread
   5 × 2 $^5/_8$ × 1 inches

7. *Neckpiece*, 1988
   Silver and 18k gold
   14 $^1/_2$ × 2 $^1/_4$ × $^1/_8$ inches
   Plate 58

8. *Neckpiece*, 1988
   Silver and 18k gold
   33 $^5/_8$ × 5 $^1/_2$ × $^1/_4$ inches

9. *Brooch*, 1989
   Stainless steel and 18k gold
   3 × 2 × $^5/_8$ inches

10. *Neckpiece with Brooch*, 1989
   Silver, 18k gold, and stainless steel
   38 × 3 × $^5/_8$ inches

11. *Brooch*, 1990
   Silver and silk
   2 $^7/_8$ × 3 $^1/_4$ × $^5/_8$ inches
   Plate 59

12. *Brooch*, 1990
   Silver and silk
   2 $^1/_2$ × 4 $^1/_8$ × $^5/_8$ inches
   Plate 59

13. *Body Piece*, 1992
   Silver, silk, semiprecious stones, stainless steel, and shell
   43 × 2 $^3/_8$ × $^7/_8$ inches
   Plate 60

14. *Body Piece*, 1993
   Nickel silver, semiprecious stones, stainless steel, copper, and 18k gold
   42 $^1/_2$ × 1 $^1/_2$ × 1 $^3/_8$ inches
   Plate 61

15. *Body Piece*, 1993
   Nickel silver, stainless steel, silver, and silk
   33 $^3/_4$ × 2 × 1 inches

16. *Body Piece (City)*, 1993
    Nickel silver, stainless steel, paper,
    silver, and shell
    30 × 10 × 1 ¹/₂ inches
    Plate 62

17. *Two Pools (Not Brooches)*, 1993
    (a) Oxidized silver
    1 ¹/₂ × 2 ³/₄ × 1 ⁵/₈ inches
    (b) Silver
    1 ¹/₂ × 2 ³/₄ × 1 ⁷/₈ inches
    Plate 63

18. *Map—Two-Part Object* from the
    Map Series, 1995
    Silver
    Each: 1 ⁷/₈ × 4 ⁷/₈ × ³/₈ inches

19. *Three Eye Brooches*, 1995
    (a) Silver and plastic
    2 ³/₄ × 2 ³/₄ × ¹/₂ inches
    (b) Silver and jade
    3 × 2 ³/₄ × ¹/₂ inches
    (c) Silver and jade
    2 ¹/₄ × 2 × ¹/₂ inches
    Plate 64

20. *Pool*, 1995
    (a) Silver and nickel silver
    2 ¹/₈ × 4 ³/₈ × ¹/₂ inches
    (b) Silver
    3 × 3 × 1 inches

21. *Pool*, 1995
    Silver, 18k gold, and cotton thread
    3 ⁵/₈ × 2 ³/₄ × ⁷/₈ inches

22. *How Many Is Four*, Nos. 1, 4, 6, 10,
    1996
    Paper, cotton thread, and silver
    Each: 8 ¹/₄ × 11 ¹/₂ inches
    Plate 65

23. *Landscape Brooch (Orchard)*, 1996
    Silver and semiprecious stones
    (a) 2 × 4 ¹/₂ × ⁷/₈ inches
    (b) 2 × 4 ¹/₂ × ³/₄ inches

24. *Landscape Brooch*, 1996
    Silver, cotton thread, and quartz
    (a) 1 ⁷/₈ × 4 ³/₈ × ³/₄ inches
    (b) 1 ³/₄ × 4 ¹/₂ × ⁵/₈ inches
    Plate 66

25. *Landscape Brooch*, 1996
    Silver, 18k gold, and tourmaline
    (a) 1 ³/₄ × 4 ³/₈ × ⁵/₈ inches
    (b) 1 ⁷/₈ × 4 ³/₈ × ⁵/₈ inches
    Plate 67

26. *Neckpiece*, 1996
    Silver, pearls, and found object
    36 ³/₄ × 3 ¹/₂ × 1 ¹/₄ inches
    Plate 68

27. *Neckpiece*, 1996
    Silver, jade, amethyst, and semi-
    precious stones
    38 ¹/₄ × 4 ¹/₄ × ³/₄ inches
    Plate 69

28. *Neckpiece with Pool*, 1996
    Silver, gilded silver, and nickel silver
    28 ¹/₂ × 3 ³/₄ × ³/₈ inches

29. *City*, 2003, from *How Many Is
    One*, 2003–2004
    Silver and semiprecious stones
    14 × 14 ³/₄ × 1 ¹/₂ inches
    Plate 70

30. *How Many Is One*, 2003–2004
    Silver, paint, and wax
    Forty-two pieces ranging from
    5 ¹/₄ × 3 ¹/₄ × ¹/₄ inches to 1 ¹/₈ × 1 ³/₄
    × ¹/₈ inches
    Plate 71

31. *Bowl*, 2003, from *How Many Is One*,
    2003–2004
    Silver
    3 ³/₄ × 6 ³/₈ × 6 ³/₈ inches
    Collection of the Racine Art
    Museum, Promised Gift of Diane
    and Jerome Phillips

32. *2 Rings*, 2005
    Silver and semiprecious stones
    (a) 1 ³/₄ × 1 ³/₁₆ × 2 inches
    (b) 1 ³/₄ × 1 × 2 inches
    Plate 72